# Pitching In A Pinch

## By Hall of Fame Pitcher, Christy Mathewson

As told first-hand dating back to Major League Baseball in the early 1900's with fascinating stories, insights, and quotes from his playing days including iconic stars Honus Wagner, Ty Cobb, Fred Clarke, Joe Tinker, "Johnny" Evers, "Chief" Meyers, "Rube" Marquard, Mordecai "Three Finger" Brown, Grover Cleveland Alexander, Orvie Overall, Ed Delahanty, "Rube" Waddell, "Slim" Sallee, "Home Run" Baker, and many other players, plus legendary Managers John McGraw and Connie Mack.

**With 100 Ballplayer Photos Added!**

### 1912 Revised Edition

Published by Baseball Classics™

Foreword by Baseball Classics Founder
# DEAN PATINO

Copyright © 2024 by Baseball Classics

All rights reserved.

The original Pitching In A Pitch by Christy Mathewson, is in the public domain. All original additions, including illustrations and written content, are copyright © 2024 by Baseball Classics and may not be reproduced in any form without written permission from the publisher or author, except permitted by United States copyright law.

Cover Art by Baseball Classics

Published by Baseball Classics

Baseball Classics © 2024
P.O. Box 911056
St. George, Utah
84791

www.BaseballClassics.com

## Dedication

*This book is dedicated to my children Ryan, Samantha, and Amanda. Their unweaving support of my relentless passion for baseball enabled me to develop and market Baseball Classics, a next generation real-time board game played by thousands of MLB fans worldwide.*

*They gave up countless hours of time for me to create products, articles, and author books to spread the greatness of America's national pastime with other fans.*

*Along this journey, besides forming their own appreciation and enthusiasm for Major League Baseball, they too helped to create Baseball Classics games throughout the decades.*

*I'm forever grateful for the beautiful, loving children they are, loving them with all my heart forevermore.*

# Pitching In A Pitch by Christy Mathewson
## Table of Contents

FOREWORD .................................................................................................5

INTRODUCTION .........................................................................................8

THE MOST DANGEROUS BATTERS I HAVE MET..............................................12

"TAKE HIM OUT"......................................................................................31

PITCHING IN A PINCH ..............................................................................62

BIG-LEAGUE PITCHERS AND THEIR PECULIARITIES. .......................................80

COACHING GOOD AND BAD ......................................................................121

HONEST AND DISHONEST SIGN STEALING ....................................................142

UMPIRES AND CLOSE DECISIONS.................................................................161

THE GAME THAT COST A PENNANT ............................................................181

WHEN THE TEAMS ARE IN SPRING TRAINING ..............................................201

JINXES AND WHAT THEY MEAN TO A BALL-PLAYER......................................223

BASE RUNNERS AND HOW THEY HELP A PITCHER TO WIN...........................244

NOTABLE INSTANCES WHERE THE "INSIDE" GAME HAS FAILED....................266

# Foreword

It's a sheer honor to publish a book originally authored in 1912 by one of the greatest pitchers Major League Baseball history has ever known to share with fans worldwide.

Christy Mathewson, known to his peers as "Matty", takes us all back in time as if we were in the dugout as he shares stories and quotes about his playing days.

He paints an authentic picture in one's mind chapter after chapter as he tells these stories of what it was like "back in the day".

Naturally, as a Baseball Hall of Famer celebrated in Cooperstown, there's been much written about Christy Mathewson.

Briefly, here is his remarkable career stat line of accomplishments spanning from 1900 to 1916 playing for the New York Giants except for a cup of coffee pitching just 1 game for the Cincinnati Reds at the end of his career.

**373 Wins vs 188 Losses for a .665 winning percentage with a dazzling 2.13 Earned Run Average (ERA), allowing only 4219 hits over 4788 2/3 innings with a skinny 1.058 WHIP (Walks + Hits / Innings Pitched). He recorded 30 or more Wins in a season 4 times and 20 or more Wins 13 times.**

**Mathewson led the National League in Wins 4 seasons, ERA 5 seasons, Strikeouts 5 seasons, and Shutouts 4 seasons.**

**During the 1908 season, Christy Mathewson completely dominated by leading the league in Wins (37), ERA (1.43), Games (56), Games Started (44), Complete Games (34), Shutouts (11), Saves (5), Innings Pitched (390 2/3), and Strikeout (259).**

**The following season in 1909, he kept batters in check leading the league with a stunningly low 1.14 ERA.**

Here's why I decided to slightly revise and publish "Pitching In A Pitch", originally authored by Mathewson in 1912.

In my humble opinion, this book should be owned and added to every avid Major League Baseball fan's home library. It's *that* good!

Besides that, why did I decide to publish it?

Especially since "Pitching In A Pitch" is readily available in the public domain with countless free eBooks available and some moderately priced soft cover books offered too.

However, when it came to getting a version in a hard cover book, my searching came up empty. Besides, there's just a small handful of photos in the original, yet his writing covers countless ballplayers, some dating back to the 1800's.

I firmly believe Christy Mathewson's efforts authoring this book deserves the respect of a hard cover version plus player photos to best tell all his firsthand stories.

This Baseball Classics book publication provides both.

Outside of a some grammatical and punctuation error corrected; this published edition keeps his language intact. There's nothing like "hearing" these stories in his voice to protect its authenticity.

In the original book, there are 4 pictures (including the headshot of Mathewson) from the original published book. Naturally, they are included here too. However, this revised edition includes 100 additional photos to include players Christy Mathewson shares his stories and insights about.

Enjoy his storytelling, dating back to Major League Baseball in the early 1900's with fascinating stories, insights, and quotes from his playing days including iconic stars Honus Wagner, Ty Cobb, Fred

Clarke, Joe Tinker, "Johnny" Evers, "Chief" Meyers, "Rube" Marquard, Mordecai "Three Finger" Brown, Grover Cleveland Alexander, Orvie Overall, Ed Delahanty, "Rube" Waddell, "Slim" Sallee, "Home Run" Baker, and dozens of other ballplayers, plus legendary Managers John McGraw and Connie Mack.

Let your mind drift back in time as Christy Mathewson paints a vivid picture of what it was like to play with and against some of the greatest players in Major League Baseball history, colorful everyday players, and a plethora of quotes as if you were there hearing them too.

You may be surprised by the similarity of today's game compared to the way it was played in the early 1900's. On the other hand, you may also be astounded how various players attempted, sometimes successfully, to win at all costs.

Mathewson speaks from the heart and takes you inside the world of Major League Baseball sharing his love and passion for the game.

There are dozens of fascinating ballplayer and managerial quotes inside that have been lifted out from long paragraphs in the original version so you can savor them all. Classic photos were added so you can get a far better idea of who he's writing about.

Enjoy reading "Pitching In A Pinch" by Hall of Fame pitcher, Christy Mathewson!

Dean Patino
Founder of Baseball Classics

# Introduction

*Written by John N. Wheeler, March, 1912 under arrangement with the publishers G. P. PUTNAM'S SONS, NEW YORK AND LONDON, The Knickerbocker Press, New York.*

Introducing a reader to Christy Mathewson seems like a superfluous piece of writing and a waste of white paper. Schoolboys of the last ten years have been acquainted with the exact figures which have made up Matty's pitching record before they had ever heard of George Washington, because George didn't play in the same League.

Perfectly good rational and normal citizens once deserted a reception to the Governor of the State because Christy Mathewson was going to pitch against the Chicago club. If the committee on arrangements wanted to make the hour of the reception earlier, all right, but no one could be expected to miss seeing Matty in the box against Chance and his Cubs for the sake of greeting the Governor.

Besides being a national hero, Matty is one of the closest students of baseball that ever came into the Big-League. By players, he has long been recognized as the greatest pitcher the game has produced. He has been pitching in the Big-Leagues for eleven years and winning games right along.

His great pitching practically won the world's championship for the Giants from the Philadelphia Athletics in 1905, and, six years later, he was responsible for one of the two victories turned in by New York pitchers in a world's series again with the Athletics.

At certain periods in his baseball career, he has pitched almost every day after the rest of the staff had fallen down. When the Giants were making their determined fight for the championship in 1908, the season that the race was finally decided by a single game with the Cubs, he worked in nine out of the last fifteen games in an effort to save his club from defeat. And he won most of them. That has always been the beauty of his pitching—his ability to win.

Matty was born in Factoryville, Pa., thirty-one years ago, and, after going to Bucknell College, he began to play ball with the Norfolk club of the Virginia League, but was soon bought by the New York Giants, where he has remained ever since and is likely to stay for some time to come, if he can continue to make himself as welcome as he has been so far. He was only nineteen when he joined the club and was a headliner from the start. Always he has been a student and something of a writer, having done newspaper work from time to time during the big series. He has made a careful study of the Big-League batters. He has kept a sort of baseball diary of his career, and, frequently, I have heard him relate unwritten chapters of baseball history filled with the thrilling incidents of his personal experience.

"Why don't you write a real book of the Big-Leaguers?" I asked him one day.

And he has done it. In this book he is telling the reader of the game as it is played in the Big-Leagues. As a college man, he is able to put his impressions of the Big-Leagues on paper graphically. It's as good as his pitching and some exciting things have happened in the Big-Leagues, stories that never found their way into the newspapers. Matty has told them. This is a true tale of Big-Leaguers, their habits and their methods of playing the game, written by one of them.

Copyright by L. Van Oeyen, Cleveland, Ohio

Made in the United States of America

# PITCHING IN A PINCH
# OR
# BASEBALL FROM THE INSIDE

## BY CHRISTOPHER MATHEWSON

## WITH A FORWARD BY BASEBALL CLASSICS FOUNDER DEAN PATINO AND INTRODUCTION BY JOHN N. WHEELER

Some Illustrations by Grosset & Dunlap
Publishers New York 1912

# The Most Dangerous Batters I Have Met

*How "Joe" Tinker Changed Overnight from a Weakling at the Plate to the Worst Batter I Had to Face—"Fred" Clarke of Pittsburg cannot be Fooled by a Change of Pace, and "Hans" Wagner's Only "Groove" Is a Base on Balls— "Inside" Information on All the Great Batters.*

**I HAVE** often been asked to which batters I have found it hardest to pitch.

It is the general impression among baseball fans that Joseph Faversham Tinker, the shortstop of the Chicago Cubs, is the worst man that I have to face in the National League. Few realize that during his first two years in the big show Joe Tinker looked like a cripple at the plate when I was pitching. His "groove" was a slow curve over the outside corner, and I fed him slow curves over that very outside corner with great regularity. Then suddenly, overnight, he became from my point of view the most dangerous batter in the League.

Christy Mathewson, New York Giants

Tinker is a clever ball-player, and one day I struck him out three times in succession with low curves over the outside corner. Instead of getting disgusted with himself, he began to think and reason. He knew that I was feeding him that low curve over the outside corner, and he started to look for an antidote. He had always taken a short, choppy swing at the ball. When he went to the clubhouse after the game in which he struck out three times, he was very quiet, so I have been told. He was just putting on his last sock when he clapped his hand to his leg and exclaimed:

"I've got it."

"Got what?" asked Johnny Evers, who happened to be sitting next to Tinker.

"Got the way to hit Matty, who had me looking as if I came from the home for the blind out there today," answered Joe.

"I should say he did," replied Evers.

"But if you've found a way to hit him, why, I'm from away out in Missouri near the Ozark Mountains." "Wait till he pitches again," said Tinker by way of conclusion, as he took his diamond ring from the trainer and left the clubhouse.

It was a four-game series in Chicago, and I had struck Tinker out three times in the first contest. McGraw decided that I should pitch the last game as well. Two men were on the bases and two were out when Tinker came to the bat for the first time in this battle, and the outfielders moved in closer for him, as he had always been what is known as a "chop" hitter. I immediately noticed something different about his style as he set himself at the plate, and then it struck me that he was standing back in the box and had a long bat. Before this he had always choked his bat short and stood up close. Now I observed that he had his stick way down by the handle.

Bresnahan was catching, and he signaled for the regular prescription for Tinker. With a lot of confidence, I handed him that old low curve. He evidently expected it, for he stepped almost across the plate, and, with that long bat, drove the ball to right field for two bases over the head of George Browne, who was playing close up to the infield, scoring both runs and eventually winning the game.

George Browne, New York Giants

"I've got your number now, Matty!" he shouted at me as he drew up at second base.

I admit that he has had it quite frequently since he switched his batting style. Now the outfielders move back when Tinker comes to the plate, for, if he connects, he hits "'em far" with that long bat. Ever since the day he adopted the "pole" he has been a thorn in my side and has broken up many a game.

That old low curve is his favorite now, and he reaches for it with the same cordiality as is displayed by an actor in reaching for his pay envelope. The only thing to do is to keep them close and try to outguess him, but Tinker is a hard man to beat at the game of wits.

Many a heady hitter in the Big-League could give the signs to the opposing pitcher, for he realizes what his weakness is and knows that a twirler is going to pitch at it. But try as hard as he will, he cannot often cover up his "groove," as Tinker did, and so he continues to be easy for the twirler who can put the ball where he wants it.

Joe Tinker, Chicago Cubs

Fred Clarke, of Pittsburg, has always been a hard man for me to fool on account of his batting form. A hitter of his type cannot be deceived by a change of pace because he stands up close to the plate, chokes his bat short, and swings left-handed. When a pitcher cannot deceive a man with a change of pace, he has to depend on curves. Let me digress briefly to explain why a change of pace will not make the ball miss Clarke's bat. He is naturally a left-field hitter and likes the ball on the outside corner of the plate. That means he swings at the ball late and makes most of his drives to left field.

How is a batter fooled by a change of pace? A pitcher gives him a speedy one and then piles a slow one right on top of it with the same motion. The batter naturally thinks it is another fast ball and swings too soon— that is, before the ball gets to him. But when a man like Clarke is at the bat and a pitcher tries to work a change of pace, what is the result? He naturally swings late and so hits a fast ball to left field. Then as the slow one comes up to the plate, he strikes at it, granted he is deceived by it, timing his swing as he would at a fast ball. If it had been a fast ball, as he thought, he would have hit it to left field, being naturally a late swinger. But on a slow one he swings clear around and pulls it to right field twice as hard as he would have hit it to left field because he has obtained that much more drive in the longer swing. Therefore, it is a rule in the profession that no left-handed batter who hits late can be deceived by a change of pace.

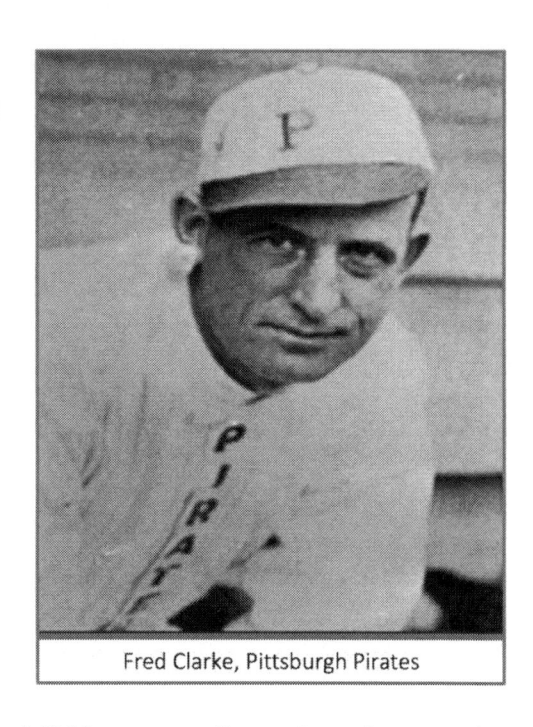

Fred Clarke, Pittsburgh Pirates

"Rube" Ellis, a left-handed hitter of the St. Louis Club, entered the League and heard complimentary stories about my pitching. Ellis came up to bat the first day that I pitched against him wondering if he would get even a foul. He was new to me and I was looking for his "groove." I gave him one over the outside corner, and he jabbed it to left field. The next time, I thought to work the change of pace, and, swinging late, he hauled the ball around to right field, and it nearly tore Fred Tenny's head off en route over first base. Five hits out of five times at bat he made off me that day, and, when he went to the clubhouse, he remarked to his teammates in this wise:

"So that is the guy who has been burning up this League, huh? We've got better 'n him in the coast circuit. He's just got the Indian sign on you. That's all."

I did a little thinking about Ellis's hitting. He used a long bat and held it down near the end and "poled 'em." He was naturally a left-field hitter and, therefore, swung late at the ball. I concluded that fast ones inside would do for Mr. Ellis, and the next time we met he

"Rube" Ellis, St. Louis Cardinals

got just those. He has been getting them ever since and now, when he makes a hit off me, he holds a celebration.

"Hans" Wagner, of Pittsburg, has always been a hard man for me, but in that I have had nothing on a lot of other pitchers. He takes a long bat, stands well back from the plate, and steps into the ball, poling it. He is what is known in baseball as a free swinger, and there are not many free swingers these days.

This is what ailed the Giants' batting during the world's series in 1911. They all attempted to become free swingers overnight and were trying to knock the ball out of the lot, instead of chopping it.

"Dan" Brouthers, Boston Reds AA

In the history of baseball there have not been more than fifteen or twenty free swingers altogether, and they are the real natural hitters of the game, the men with eyes nice enough and accurate enough to take a long wallop at the ball. "Dan" Brouthers was one, and so was "Cap" Anson. Sherwood Magee and "Hans" Wagner are contemporary free swingers. Men of this type wield a heavy bat as if it were a toothpick and step back and forth in the box, hitting the ball on any end of the plate. Sometimes it is almost impossible to pass a man of this sort purposely, for a little carelessness in getting the ball too close to the plate may result in his stepping up and hitting it a mile. Pitchers have been searching for Wagner's "groove" for years, and, if any one of them has located it, he has his discovery copyrighted, for I never heard of it.

Only one pitcher, that I can recall, always had it on Wagner, and that man was Arthur Raymond, sometimes called "Bugs." He seemed to upset the German by his careless manner in the box and by his "kidding" tactics. I have seen him make Wagner go after bad balls, a thing that "Hans" seldom can be induced to do by other twirlers.

I remember well the first time I pitched against Wagner. Jack Warner was catching, and I, young and new in the League, had spent a lot of time with him, learning the weaknesses of the batters and being coached as to how to treat them. Wagner loomed up at the bat in a pinch, and I could not remember what Warner had said about his flaw. I walked out of the box to confer with the catcher.

"What's his 'groove,' Jack?" I asked him.

"A base on balls," replied Warner, without cracking a smile.

That's always been Wagner's "groove."

There used to be a player on the Boston team named Claude Ritchey who "had it on me" for some reason or other. He was a left-handed hitter and naturally drove the ball to left field, so that I could not fool him with a change of pace. He was always able to outguess me in a pinch and seemed to know by intuition what was coming.

Claude Ritchey, Boston Doves

There has been for a long time an ardent follower of the Giants named Mrs. Wilson, who raves wildly at a game, and is brokenhearted when the team loses. The Giants were playing in Boston one day and needed the game very badly. It was back in 1905, at the time the club could clinch the pennant by winning one contest, and the flag-assuring game is the hardest one to win. Two men got on the bases in the ninth inning with the score tied and no one out. The crowd was stamping its feet and hooting madly, trying to rattle me. I heard Mrs. Wilson shrill loudly above the noise:

"Stick with them, Matty!"

Ritchey came up to the bat, and I passed him purposely, trying to get him to strike at a bad ball. I wouldn't take a chance on letting him hit at a good one. Mrs. Wilson thought I was losing my control, and unable to stand it any longer she got up and walked out of the grounds.

Then I fanned the next two batters, and the last man hit a roller to Devlin and was thrown out at first base. I was told afterwards that Mrs. Wilson stood outside the ground, waiting to hear the crowd cheer, which would have told her it was all over.

She lingered at the gate until the fourteenth inning, fearing to return because she expected to see us routed. At last, she heard a groan from the home crowd when we won in the fourteenth. Still, she would not believe that I had weathered the storm and won the game that gave the Giants a pennant, but waited to be assured by some of the spectators leaving the grounds before she came around to congratulate us.

All batters who are good waiters, and will not hit at bad balls, are hard to deceive, because it means a twirler has to lay the ball over, and then the hitter always has the better chance. A pitcher will try to get a man to hit at a bad ball before he will put it near the plate.

Many persons have asked me why I do not use my "fade-away" oftener when it is so effective, and the only answer is that every time I throw the "fade-away" it takes so much out of my arm. It is a very hard ball to deliver. Pitching it ten or twelve times in a game kills my arm, so I save it for the pinches.

Many fans do not know what this ball really is. It is a slow curve pitched with the motion of a fast ball. But most curve balls break away from a right-handed batter a little. The fade-away breaks toward him.

Baker, of the Athletics, is one of the most dangerous hitters I have ever faced, and we were not warned to look out for him before the 1911 world's series, either. Certain friends of the Giants gave us some "inside" information on the Athletics' hitters. Among others, the Cubs supplied us with good tips, but no one spread the Baker alarm. I was told to watch out for Collins as a dangerous man, one who was likely to break up a game any time with a long drive.

I consider Baker one of the hardest, cleanest hitters I have ever faced, and he drives the ball on a line to any field. The fielders cannot play for him. He did not show up well in the first game of the world's series because the Athletics thought they were getting our signs, and we crossed Baker with two men on the bases in the third inning. He lost a chance to be a hero right there.

The roughest deal that I got from Baker in the 1911 series was in the third game, which was the second in New York. We had made one run and the ninth inning rolled around with the Giants still leading, 1 to 0. The first man at the bat grounded out and then Baker came up. I realized by this time that he was a hard proposition but figured that he could not hit a low curve over the outside corner, as he is naturally a right-field hitter. I got one ball and one strike on him and then delivered a ball that was aimed to be a low curve over the outside corner. Baker refused to swing at it, and Brennan, the umpire, called it a ball.

Frank "Home Run" Baker, Philadelphia A's

I thought that it caught the outside corner of the plate, and that Brennan missed the strike. It put me in the hole with the count two balls and one strike, and I had to lay the next one over very near the middle to keep the count from being three and one. I pitched a curve ball that was meant for the outside corner but cut the plate better than I intended. Baker stepped up into it and smashed it into the grand-stand in right field for a home run, and there is the history of that famous wallop. This tied the score.

A pitcher has two types of batters to face. One is the man who is always thinking and guessing and waiting, trying to get the pitcher in the hole. Evers, of the Cubs, is that sort. They tell me that "Ty" Cobb of Detroit is the most highly developed of this type of hitter. I have never seen him play. Then the other kind is the natural slugger, who does not wait for anything, and who could not outguess a pitcher if he did. The brainy man is the harder for a pitcher to face because he is a constant source of worry.

There are two ways of fooling a batter. One is literally to "mix 'em up," and the other is to keep feeding him the same sort of a ball, but to induce him to think that something else is coming. When a brainy man is at the bat, he is always trying to figure out what to expect. If he knows, then his chances of getting a hit are greatly increased. For instance, if a batter has two balls and two strikes on him, he naturally concludes that the pitcher will throw him a curve ball and prepares for it. Big-League ballplayers recognize only two kinds of pitched balls—the curve and the straight one.

When a catcher in the Big-League signals for a curved ball, he means a drop, and, after handling a certain pitcher for a time, he gets to know just how much the ball is going to curve. That is why the one catcher receives for the same pitcher so regularly, because they get to work together harmoniously. "Chief" Meyers, the big Indian catcher on the Giants, understands my style so well that in some games he hardly has to give a sign. But, oddly enough, he could never catch Raymond because he did not like to handle the spit ball, a hard delivery to receive, and Raymond and he could not get along together as a battery. They would cross each other. But Arthur Wilson caught Raymond almost perfectly. This explains the loss of effectiveness of many pitchers when a certain catcher is laid up or out of the game.

"Cy" Seymour, formerly the outfielder of the Giants, was one of the hardest batters I ever had to pitch against when he was with the Cincinnati club and going at the top of his stride. He liked a curved ball, and could hit it hard and far, and was always waiting for it. He was very clever at out-guessing a pitcher and being able to conclude what was coming. For a

"Cy" Seymour, Cincinnati Reds

long time whenever I pitched against him I had "mixed 'em up" literally, handing him first a fast ball and then a slow curve and so on, trying to fool him in this way. But one day we were playing in Cincinnati, and I decided to keep delivering the same kind of a ball, that old fast one around his neck, and to try to induce him to believe that a curve was coming. I pitched him nothing but fast ones that day, and he was always waiting for a curve. The result was that I had him in the hole all the time, and I struck him out three times. He has never gotten over it.

Only recently I saw Seymour, and he said: "Matty, you are the only man that ever struck me out three times in the same game."

He soon guessed, however, that I was not really mixing them up, and then I had to switch my style again for him. Some pitchers talk to batters a great deal, hoping to get their minds off the game in this way, and thus be able to sneak strikes over. But I find that talking to a batter disconcerts me almost as much as it does him, and I seldom do it. Repartee is not my line anyway.

Bender talked to the Giant players all through that first game in the 1911 world's series, the one in which he wore the smile, probably because he was a pitcher old in the game and several of the younger men on the New York team acted as if they were nervous. Snodgrass and the Indian kept up a running fire of small talk every time that the Giants' center-fielder came to the plate.

Snodgrass got hit by pitched balls twice, and this seemed to worry Bender. When the New York center-fielder came to the bat in the eighth inning, the Indian showed his even teeth in the chronic grin and greeted Snodgrass in this way: "Look out, Freddie, you don't get hit this time."

Then Bender wound up and with all his speed drove the ball straight at Snodgrass's head, and Bender had more speed in that first game than I ever saw him use before. Snodgrass dodged, and the ball drove into Thomas's glove. This pitching the first ball at the head of a batter is an old trick of pitchers when they think a player intends to get hit purposely or that he is crowding the plate.

"Chief" Bender, Philadelphia Athletics

"If you can't push 'em over better than that," retorted Snodgrass, "I won't need to get hit. Let's see your fast one now."

"Try this one," suggested Bender, as he pitched another fast one that cut the heart of the plate.

Snodgrass swung and hit nothing but the air. The old atmosphere was very much mauled by bats in that game anyway.

"You missed that one a mile, Freddie," chuckled the Indian, with his grin.

Snodgrass eventually struck out and then Bender broke into a laugh.

"You ain't a batter, Freddie," exclaimed the Indian, as he

walked to the bench. "You're a backstop. You can never get anywhere without being hit."

If a pitcher is going to talk to a batter, he must size up his man. An irritable, nervous young player often will fall for the conversation, but most seasoned hitters will not answer back. The Athletics, other than Bender, will not talk in a game. We tried to get after them in the first contest in 1911, and we could not get a rise out of one of them, except when Snodgrass spiked Baker, and I want to say right here that this much discussed incident was accidental. Baker was blocking Snodgrass out, and the New York player had a perfect right to the base line.

Sherwood Magee of the Philadelphia National League team is one of the hardest batters that I ever have had to face, because he has a great eye, and is of the type of free swingers who take a mad wallop at the ball and are always liable to break up a game with a long drive. Just once I talked to him when he was at the bat, more because we were both worked up than for any other reason, and he came out second best. It was while the Giants were playing at American League Park in 1911 after the old Polo Grounds had burned. Welchonce, who was the center-fielder for the Phillies at the time, hit a slow one down the first base line, and I ran over to field the ball. I picked it up as the runner arrived and had no time to straighten up to dodge him. So, I struck out my shoulder and he ran into it. There was no other way to make the play, but I guess it looked bad from the stand, because Welchonce fell down.

Magee came up to bat next, threw his hat on the ground, and started to call me names. He is bad when irritated—and tolerably easy to irritate, as shown by the way in which he knocked down Finnegan, the umpire, last season because their ideas on a strike differed slightly. I replied on that occasion but remembered to keep the ball away from the center of the plate. That is about all I did do, but he was more wrought up than I and hit only a slow grounder to the infield. He was out by several feet. He took a wild slide at the bag, however, feet first, in what looked like an attempt to spike Merkle. We talked some more after that, but it has all been forgotten now.

Sherwood Magee, Philadelphia Phillies

To be a successful pitcher in the Big-League, a man must have the head and the arm. When I first joined the Giants, I had what is known as the "old round-house curve," which is no more than a big, slow outdrop. I had been fooling them in the minor leagues with it, and I was somewhat chagrined when George Davis, then the manager of the club, came to me and told me to forget the curve, as it would be of no use. It was then that I began to develop my drop ball.

A pitcher must watch all the time for any little unconscious motion before he delivers the ball. If a base runner can guess just when he is going to pitch, he can get a much better start. Drucke used to have a little motion with his foot just before he pitched, of which he himself was entirely unconscious, but the other clubs got on to it and stole bases on him wildly. McGraw has since broken him of it.

The Athletics say that I make a motion peculiar to the fade-away. Some spit-ball pitchers announce when they are going to throw a moist one by looking at the ball as they dampen it. At other times, when they "stall," they do not look at the ball. The Big-League batter is watching for all these little things and, if a pitcher is not careful, he will find a lot of men who are hard to pitch to. There are plenty anyway, and, as a man grows older, this number increases season by season.

# "Take Him Out"

*Many a Pitcher's Heart has been Broken by the Cry from the Stands, "Take Him Out"—Russell Ford of the New York Yankees was Once Beaten by a Few Foolish Words Whispered into the Batter's Ear at a Critical Moment—Why "Rube" Marquard Failed for Two Years to be a Big-Leaguer—The Art of Breaking a Pitcher into Fast Company.*

**A PITCHER** is in a tight game, and the batter makes a hit. Another follows and some fan back in the stand cries in stentorian tones: "Take him out!"

It is the dirge of baseball which has broken the hearts of pitchers ever since the game began and will continue to do so as long as it lives. Another fan takes up the shout, and another, and another, until it is a chorus.

"Take him out! Take him out! Take him out!"

The pitcher has to grin, but that constant cry is wearing on nerves strung to the breaking point. The crowd is against him, and the next batter hits, and a run scores. The manager stops the game, beckons to the pitcher from the bench, and he has to walk away from the box, facing the crowd—not the team—which has beaten him. It is the psychology of baseball.

Some foolish words once whispered into the ear of a batter by a clever manager in the crisis of one of the closest games ever played in baseball turned the tide and unbalanced a pitcher who had been working like a perfectly adjusted machine through seven terrific innings. That is also the "psychology of pitching." The man wasn't beaten because he weakened, because he lost his grip, because of any physical deficiency, but because some foolish words—words that meant nothing, had nothing to do with the game—had upset his mental attitude.

The game was the first one played between the Giants and the Yankees in the post-season series of 1910, the batter was Bridwell, the manager was John McGraw, and the pitcher, Russell Ford of the Yankees. The cast of characters having been named; the story may now enter the block.

Spectators who recall the game will remember that the two clubs had been battling through the early innings with neither team able to gain an advantage, and the Giants came to bat for the eighth inning with the score a tie. Ford was pitching perfectly with all the art of a master craftsman. Each team had made one run. I was the first man up and started the eighth inning with a single because Ford slackened up a little against me, thinking that I was not dangerous. Devore beat out an infield hit, and Doyle bunted and was safe, filling the bases. Then Ford went to work. He struck out Snodgrass, and Hemphill caught Murray's fly far too near the infield to permit me to try to score. It looked as if Ford were going to get out of the hole when "Al" Bridwell, the former Giant shortstop, came to the bat. Ford threw him two bad balls, and then McGraw ran out from the bench, and, with an autocratic finger, held up the game while he whispered into Bridwell's ear.

"Al" nodded knowingly, and the whole thing was a pantomime, a wordless play, that made Sumurun look like a bush-league production. Bridwell stepped back into the batter's box, and McGraw returned to the bench. On the next pitch, "Al" was hit in the leg and went to first base, forcing the run that broke the tie across the plate. That run also broke Ford's heart.

John McGraw, New York Giants

And here is what McGraw whispered into the attentive ear of Bridwell: "How many quail did you say you shot when you were hunting last fall, Al?"

John McGraw, the psychologist, baseball general and manager, had heard opportunity knock. With his fingers on the pulse of the game, he had felt the tenseness of the situation, and realized, all in the flash of an eye, that

Ford was wabbling and that anything would push him over. He stopped the game and whispered into Bridwell's ear while Ford was feeling more and more the intensity of the crisis. He had an opportunity to observe the three men on the bases. He wondered what McGraw was whispering, what trick was to be expected. Was he telling the batter to get hit? Yes, he must be. Then he did just that—hit the batter and lost the game.

Why can certain pitchers always beat certain clubs and why do they look like bush leaguers against others? To be concrete, why can Brooklyn fight Chicago so hard and look foolish playing against the Giants? Why can the Yankees take game after game from Detroit and be easy picking for the Cleveland club in most of their games? Why does Boston beat Marquard when he can make the hard Philadelphia hitters look like blind men with bats in their hands? Why could I beat Cincinnati game after game for two years when the club was filled with hard hitters? It is the psychology of baseball, the mental attitudes of the players, some intangible thing that works on the mind. Managers are learning to use this subtle, indescribable element which is such a factor.

The great question which confronts every Big-League manager is how to break a valuable young pitcher into the game. "Rube" Marquard came to the Giants in the fall of 1908 out of the American Association heralded as a world-beater, with a reputation that shimmered and shone. The newspapers were crowded with stories of the man for whom McGraw had paid $11,000, who had been standing them on their heads in the West, who had curves that couldn't be touched, and was a bargain at the unheard-of price paid for him.

"Rube" Marquard came to the Giants in a burst of glory and publicity when the club was fighting for the pennant. McGraw was up against it for pitchers at that time, and one win, turned in by a young pitcher, might have resulted in the Giants winning the pennant as the season ended.

"Don't you think Marquard would win? Can't you put him in?" Mr. Brush, the owner of the club, asked McGraw one day when he was discussing the pitching situation with the manager.

"I don't know," answered McGraw. "If he wins his first time out in the Big-Leagues, he will be a world-beater, and, if he loses, it may cost us a good pitcher."

But Mr. Brush was insistent. Here a big price had been paid for a pitcher with a record, and pitchers were what the club needed. The newspapers declared that the fans should get a look at this "$11,000 beauty" in action. A double header was scheduled to be played with the Cincinnati club in the month of September, in 1908, and the pitching staff was gone. McGraw glanced over his collection of crippled and worked-out twirlers. Then he saw "Rube" Marquard, big and fresh.

"Go in and pitch," he ordered after Marquard had warmed up.

McGraw always does things that way, makes up his mind about the most important matters in a minute and then stands by his judgment. Marquard went into the box, but he didn't pitch much. He has told me about it since.

"When I saw that crowd, Matty," he said, "I didn't know where I was. It looked so big to me, and they were all wondering what I was going to do, and all thinking that McGraw had paid $11,000 for me, and now they were to find out whether he had gotten stuck, whether he had picked up a gold brick with the plating on it very thin. I was wondering, myself, whether I would make good."

"Rube" Marquard, New York Giants

What Marquard did that day is a matter of record, public property, like marriage and death notices. Kane, the little rightfielder on the Cincinnati club, was the first man up, and, although he was one of the smallest targets in the league, Marquard hit him. He promptly stole second, which worried "Rube" some more. Up came Lobert, the man who broke Marquard's heart.

"Now we'll see," said Lobert to "Rube," as he advanced to the plate, "whether you're a busher."

Then Lobert, the tantalizing Teuton with the bow-legs, whacked out a triple to the far outfield and stopped at third with a mocking smile on his face which would have gotten the late Job's goat.

"You're identified," said "Hans"; "you're a busher."

Some fan shouted the fatal "Take him out."

Marquard was gone. Bescher followed with another triple, and, after that, the official scorer got writer's cramp trying to keep track of the hits and runs. The number of hits, I don't think, ever was computed with any great amount of exactitude. Marquard was taken out of the box in the fifth inning, and he was two years recovering from the shock of that beating. McGraw had put him into the game against his better judgment, and he paid for it dearly.

Marquard had to be nursed along on the bench finishing games, starting only against easy clubs, and learning the ropes of the Big-Leagues before he was able to be a winning pitcher. McGraw was a long time realizing on his investment. All Marquard needed was a victory, a decisive win, over a strong club.

Photo by L. Van Oeyen, Cleveland, Ohio
Ty Cobb and Hans Wagner

"An American and National League star of the first magnitude. Fans of the rival leagues never tire of discussing the relative merits of these two great players. Both are always willing to take a chance and seem to do their best work when pressed hardest."

The Giants played a disastrous series with the Philadelphia club early in July, 1911, and lost four games straight. All the pitchers were shot to pieces, and the Quakers seemed to be unbeatable. McGraw was at a loss for a man to use in the fifth game. The weather was steaming hot, and the players were dragged out, while the pitching staff had lost all its starch. As McGraw's eye scanned his bedraggled talent, Marquard, reading his thoughts, walked up to him.

"Give me a chance," he asked.

"Go in," answered McGraw, again making up his mind on the spur of the moment.

Marquard went into the game and made the Philadelphia batters, whose averages had been growing corpulent on the pitching of the rest of the staff, look foolish. There on that sweltering July afternoon, when everything steamed in the blistering heat, a pitcher was being born again. Marquard had found himself, and, for the rest of the season, he was strongest against the Philadelphia team, for it had been that club which restored his confidence.

There is a sequel to that old Lobert incident, too. In one of the last series in Philadelphia, toward the end of the season, Marquard and Lobert faced each other again.

Said Marquard: "Remember the time, you bow-legged Dutchman, when you asked me whether I was a busher? Here is where I pay you back. This is the place where you get a bad showing up."

And he fanned Lobert—whiff! whiff! whiff!—like that. He became the greatest lefthander in the country, and would have been sooner, except for the enormous price paid for him and the widespread publicity he received, which caused him to be over-anxious to make good. It's the psychology of the game.

"You can't hit what you don't see," says "Joe" Tinker of Marquard's pitching. "When he throws his fast one, the only way you know it's past you is because you hear the ball hit the catcher's glove."

Fred Clarke, of the Pittsburg club, was up against the same proposition when he purchased "Marty" O'Toole for $22,500 in 1911. The newspapers of the country were filled with figures and pictures of the real estate and automobiles that could be bought with the same amount of money, lined up alongside of pictures of O'Toole, as when the comparative strengths of the navies of the world are shown by placing different sizes of battleships in a row, or when the length of the *Lusitania* is emphasized by printing a picture of it balancing gracefully on its stern alongside the Singer Building.

Clarke realized that he had all this publicity with which to contend, and that it would do his expensive new piece of pitching bric-à-brac no good. O'Toole, jerked out of a minor league where he had been pitching quietly, along with his name in ten or a dozen papers, was suddenly a national figure, measuring up in newspaper space with Roosevelt and Taft and J. Johnson.

When O'Toole joined the Pirates near the end of the season, Clarke knew down in his heart the club had no chance of winning the pennant with Wagner hurt, although he still publicly declared he was in the race. He did not risk jumping O'Toole right into the game as soon as he reported and taking the chance of breaking his heart. Opposing players, if they are up in the pennant hunt, are hard on a pitcher of this sort and would lose no opportunity to mention the price paid for

"Marty" O'Toole, Pittsburgh Pirates

him and connect it pointedly with his showing, if that showing was a little wobbly. Charity begins at home, and stays there, in the Big-Leagues. At least, I never saw any of it on the ball fields, especially if the club is in the race, and the only thing that stands between it and a victory is the ruining of a $22,500 pitcher of a rival.

Clarke nursed O'Toole along on the bench for a couple of weeks until he got to be thoroughly acclimated, and then he started him in a game against Boston, the weakest club in the league, after he had sent for Kelly, O'Toole's regular catcher, to inspire more confidence. O'Toole had an easy time of it at his Big-League début, for the Boston players did not pick on him any to speak of, as they were not a very hard bunch of pickers. The Pittsburg team gave him a nice comfortable, cozy lead, and he was pitching along ahead of the game all the way.

In the fifth or sixth inning Clarke slipped Gibson, the regular Pittsburg catcher, behind the bat, and O'Toole had won his first game in the Big-League before he knew it. He then reasoned I have won here. I belong here. I can get along here. It isn't much different from the crowd I came from, except for the name, and that's nothing to get timid about if I can clean up as easily as I did to-day.

Fred Clarke, also a psychologist and baseball manager, had worked a valuable pitcher into the League, and he had won his first game. If he had started him against some club like the Giants, for instance, where he would have had to face a big crowd and the conversation and spirit of players who were after a pennant and hot after it, he might have lost and his heart would have been broken. Successfully breaking into the game an expensive pitcher, who has cost a club a large price, is one of the hardest problems which confronts a manager. Now O'Toole is all right if he has the pitching goods. He has taken his initial plunge, and all he has to do is to make good next year. The psychology element is eliminated from now on.

I have been told that Clarke was the most relieved man in seven counties when O'Toole came through with that victory in Boston.

"I had in mind all the time," said Fred, "what happened to McGraw when he was trying to introduce Marquard into the smart set, and I was afraid the same thing would happen to me. I had a lot of confidence in the nerve of that young fellow though, because he stood up well under fire the first day he got into Pittsburg. One of those lady reporters was down to the club offices to meet him the morning he got into town, and they always kind of have me, an old campaigner, stepping away from the plate. She pulled her pad and pencil on Marty first thing, before he had had a chance to knock the dirt out of his cleats, and said:

"'Now tell me about yourself.'

"He stepped right into that one, instead of backing away. "'What do you want me to tell?' he asks her.

"Then I knew he was all right. He was there with the 'come-back.'"

But the ideal way to break a star into the Big-League is that which marked the entrance of Grover Cleveland Alexander, of the Philadelphia club. The Cincinnati club had had its eye on Alexander for some time, but "Tacks" Ashenbach, the scout, now dead, had advised against him, declaring that he would be no good against "regular batters." Philadelphia got him at the waiver price and he was among the lot in the newspapers marked "Those who also joined." He started out in 1911 and won two or three games before anyone paid any attention to him. Then he kept on winning until one manager was saying to another:

"That guy, Alexander, is a hard one to beat."

He had won ten or a dozen games before it was fully realized that he was a star. Then he was so accustomed to the Big-League he acted as if he had been living in it all his life, and there was no getting on his nerves. When he started, he had everything to gain and nothing to lose. If he didn't last, the newspapers wouldn't laugh at him, and the people wouldn't say:

Grover Cleveland Alexander, Philadelphia A's

"$11,000, or $22,500, for a lemon." That's the dread of all ball players.

Such is the psychology of introducing promising pitchers into the Big-Leagues. The Alexander route is the ideal one, but it's hard to get stars now without paying enormous prices for them. Philadelphia was lucky.

There is another element which enters into all forms of athletics. Tennis players call it nervousness, and ball players, in the frankness of the game, call it a "yellow streak." It is the inability to stand the gaff, the weakening in the pinches. It is something ingrained in a man that can't be cured. It is the desire to quit when the situation is serious. It is different from stage fright, because a man may get over that, but a "yellow streak" is always with him. When a new player breaks into the League, he is put to the most severe test by the other men to see if he is "yellow." If he is found wanting, he is hopeless in the Big-League, for the news will spread, and he will receive no quarter. It is the cardinal sin in a ball player.

"Hans" Wagner, Pittsburgh Pirates

For some time after "Hans" Wagner's poor showing in the world's series of 1903, when the Pittsburg club was defeated for the World's Championship by the Boston American League club, it was reported that he was "yellow." This grieved the Dutchman deeply, for I don't know a ball player in either league who would assay less quit to the ton than Wagner. He is always there and always fighting. Wagner felt the inference which his teammates drew very keenly. This was the real tragedy in Wagner's career. Notwithstanding his stolid appearance, he is a sensitive player, and this hurt him more than anything else in his life ever has.

When the Pittsburg club played Detroit in 1909 for the championship of the world, many, even of Wagner's admirers, said, "The Dutchman will quit." It was in this series he vindicated himself. His batting scored the majority of the Pittsburg runs, and his fielding was little short of wonderful. He was demonstrating his gameness. Many men would have quit under the reflection. They would have been unable to withstand the criticism, but not Wagner.

Many persons implied that John Murray, the rightfielder on the Giants, was "yellow" at the conclusion of the 1911 world's series because, after batting almost three hundred in the season, he did not get a hit in the six games. But there isn't a man on the team gamer. He hasn't any nerves. He's one of the sort of ball players who says:

"Well, now I've got my chew of tobacco in my mouth. Let her go."

There is an interesting bit of psychology connected with Wagner and the spitball. It comes as near being Wagner's "groove" as any curve that has found its way into the Big-Leagues. This is explained by the fact that the first time Wagner ever faced "Bugs" Raymond he didn't get a hit with Arthur using the spitter.

Consequently, the report went around the circuit that Wagner couldn't hit the spitball. He disproved this theory against two or three spit-ball pitchers, but as long as Raymond remained in the League he had it on the hard-hitting Dutchman.

"Here comes a 'spitter,' Hans. Look out for it," Raymond would warn Wagner, with a wide grin, and then he would pop up a wet one.

"Guess I'll repeat on that dose, Hans; you didn't like that one."

"Bugs" Raymond, New York Giants

And Wagner would get so worked up that he frequently struck out against "Bugs" when the rest of his club was hitting the eccentric pitcher hard. It was because he achieved the idea on the first day he couldn't hit the spit-ball, and he wasn't able to rid his mind of the impression. Many fans often wondered why Raymond had it on Wagner, the man whose only "groove" is a base on balls. "Bugs" had the edge after that first day when Wagner lost confidence in his ability to hit the spit-ball as served by Raymond.

In direct contrast to this loss of confidence on Wagner's part was the incident attendant upon Arthur Devlin's debut into the Big-League. He had joined the club a youngster, in the season of 1904, and McGraw had not counted upon him to play third base, having planned to plant Bresnahan at that corner. But Bresnahan developed sciatic rheumatism early in the season, and Devlin was put on the bag in the emergency with a great deal of misgiving.

The first day he was in the game he came up to the bat with the bases full. The Giants were playing Brooklyn at the Polo Grounds, and two men had already struck out, with the team two runs behind. Devlin came out from the bench.

"Who is this youthful-looking party?" one fan asked another, as they scanned their score cards.

"Devlin, some busher, taking Bresnahan's place," another answered.

"Well, it's all off now," was the general verdict.

The crowd settled back, and one could feel the lassitude in the atmosphere. But Devlin had his first chance to make good in a pinch. There was no weariness in his manner. Poole, the Brooklyn pitcher, showing less respect than he should have for the newcomer in baseball society, spilled one over too near the middle, and Arthur drove out a home run, winning the game.

Those who had refused to place any confidence in him only a moment before, were on their feet cheering wildly now. And Devlin played third base for almost eight years after that, and none thought of Bresnahan and his rheumatism until he began catching again. Devlin, after that home run, was oozing confidence from every pore and burned up the League with his batting for three years. He got the old confidence from his start. The fans had expected nothing from him, and he had delivered. He had gained everything. He had made the most dramatic play in baseball on his first day, a home run with the bases full.

When Fred Snodgrass first started playing as a regular with the Giants about the middle of the season of 1910, he hit any ball pitched him hard and had all the fans marveling at his stick work. He believed that he could hit anything and, as long as he retained that belief, he could. But the Chalmers Automobile Company had offered a prize of one nice, mild-mannered motor car to the batter in either league who finished the season with the biggest average.

Fred Snodgrass, New York Giants

Snodgrass was batting over four hundred at one time and was ahead of them all when suddenly the New York evening papers began to publish the daily averages of the leaders for the automobile, boosting Snodgrass. It suddenly struck Fred that he was a great batter and that to keep his place in that daily standing he would have to make a hit every time he went to the plate. These printed figures worried him. His batting fell off miserably until, in the post season series with the Yankees, he gave one of the worst exhibitions of any man on the team.

The newspapers did it.

"They got me worrying about myself," he told me once.

"I began to think how close I was to the car and had a moving picture of myself driving it. That settled it."

Many promising young players are broken in their first game in the Big-League by the ragging which they are forced to undergo at the hands of veteran catchers. John Kling is a very bad man with youngsters, and sometimes he can get on the nerves of older players in close games when the nerves are strung tight. The purpose of a catcher in talking to a man in this way is to distract his attention from batting, and once this is accomplished, he is gone. A favorite trick of a catcher is to say to a new batter:

"Look out for this fellow. He's got a mean 'bean' ball, and he hasn't any influence over it. There's a poor 'boob' in the hospital now that stopped one with his head." Then the catcher signs for the pitcher to throw the next one at the young batter's head. If he pulls away, an unpardonable sin in baseball, the dose is repeated.

"Yer almost had your foot in the water-pail over by the bench that time," says the catcher.

Bing! Up comes another "beaner." Then, after the catcher has sized the new man up, he makes his report. "He won't do. He's yellow."

And the players keep mercilessly after this shortcoming, this ingrained fault which, unlike a mechanical error, cannot be corrected until the new player is driven out of the League.

Perhaps the catcher says: "He's game, that guy. No scare to him."

After that he is let alone. It's the psychology of batting.

Once, when I first broke into the League, Jack Chesbro, then with Pittsburg, threw a fast one up, and it went behind my head, although I tried to dodge back. He had lots of speed in those days, too. It set me wondering what would have happened if the ball had hit me. The more I thought, the more it struck me that it would have greatly altered my face had it gotten into the course of the ball. Ever afterwards, he had it on me, and, for months, a fast one at the head had me backing away from the plate.

Jack Chesbro, Pittsburgh Pirates

In contrast to this experience of mine was the curing of "Josh" Devore, the leftfielder of the Giants, of being bat shy against left-handers. Devore has always been very weak at the bat with a southpaw in the box, dragging his right foot away from the plate. This was particularly the case against "Slim" Sallee, the tenuous southpaw of the St. Louis Nationals. Finally, McGraw, exasperated after "Josh" had struck out twice in one day, said:

"That fellow hasn't got speed enough to bend a pane of glass at the home plate throwing from the box, and you're pullin' away as if he was shooting them out of a gun. It's a crime to let him beat you. Go up there the next time and get hit and see if he can hurt you. If you don't get hit, you're fined $10."

Devore, who is as fond of $10 as the next one, went to the bat and took one of Sallee's slants in a place where it would do the least damage.

He trotted to first base smiling. "What'd I tell you?" asked McGraw, coaching. "Could he hurt you?"

"Say," replied "Josh," "I'd hire out to let them pitch baseballs at me if none could throw harder than that guy."

Devore was cured of being bat shy when Sallee was pitching, right then and there, and he has improved greatly against all left-handers ever since, so much so that McGraw leaves him in the game now when a southpaw pitches, instead of placing Beals Becker in left field as he used to. All Devore needed was the confidence to stand up to the plate against them, to rid his mind of the idea that, if once he got hit, he would leave the field feet first. That slam in the slats which Sallee handed him supplied the confidence.

"Josh" Devore, New York Giants

When Devore was going to Philadelphia for the second game of the world's series in the fall of 1911, the first one in the other town, he was introduced to "Ty" Cobb, the Detroit out-fielder, by some newspaper man on the train, and, as it was the first time Devore had ever met Cobb, he sat down with him and they talked all the way over.

"Gee," said "Josh" to me, as we were getting off the train, "that fellow Cobb knows a lot about batting. He told me some things about the American League pitchers just now, and he didn't know he was doing it. I never let on. But I just hope that fellow Plank works to-day, if they think that I am weak against left-handers. Say, Matty, I could write a book about that guy and his 'grooves' now, after buzzing Cobb, and the funny thing is he didn't know he was telling me."

Plank pitched that day and fanned Devore four times out of a possible four. "Josh" didn't even get a foul off him.

"Thought you knew all about that fellow," I said to Devore after the game.

"I've learned since that Cobb and he are pretty thick," replied "Josh," "and I guess 'Ty' was giving me a bad steer."

It was evident that Cobb had been filling "Josh" up with misinformation that was working around in Devore's mind when he went to the plate to face Plank, and, instead of being open to impressions, these wrong opinions had already been planted and he was constantly trying to confirm them. Plank was crossing him all the time, and being naturally weak against left-handers, this additional handicap made Devore look foolish.

Eddie Plank, Philadelphia Athletics

In the well-worn words of Mr. Dooley, it has been my experience "to trust your friends but cut the cards." By that, I mean one ball player will often come to another with a tip that he really thinks worthwhile, but that avails nothing in the end. A man has to be a pretty smart ball player to dispense accurate information about others, because the Big-Leaguers know their own "grooves" and are naturally trying to cover them up. Then a batter may be weak against one pitcher on a certain kind of a ball, and may whale the same sort of delivery, with a different twist to it, out of the lot against another.

That was the experience I had with "Ed" Delahanty, the famous slugger of the old Philadelphia National League team, who is now dead. During my first year in the League several well-meaning advisers came to me and said:

"Don't give 'Del' any high fast ones because, if you do, you will just wear your fielders out worse than a George M. Cohan show does the chorus. They will think they are in a Marathon race instead of a ball game."

Being young, I took this advice, and the first time I pitched against Delahanty, I fed him curved balls. He hit these so far, the first two times he came to bat that one of the balls was never found, and everybody felt like shaking hands with Van Haltren, the old Giant outfielder, when he returned with the other, as if he had been away on a vacation some place. In fact, I had been warned against giving any of this Philadelphia team of sluggers high fast ones, and I had been delivering a diet of curves to all of them which they were sending to the limits of the park and further, with great regularity. At last, when Delahanty came to the bat for the third time in the game, Van Haltren walked into the box from the outfield and handed the ball to me, after he had just gone to the fence to get it. Elmer Flick had hit it there.

"Matty," he pleaded, "for the love of Mike, slip this fellow a base on balls and let me get my wind."

Instead, I decided to switch my style, and I fed Delahanty high fast ones, the dangerous dose, and he struck out then and later. He wasn't expecting them and was so surprised that he couldn't hit the ball. Only two of the six balls at which he struck were good ones. I found out afterwards that the tradition about not delivering any high fast balls to the Philadelphia hitters was the outgrowth of the old buzzer tipping service, established in 1899, by which the batters were informed what to expect by Morgan Murphy, located in the clubhouse with a pair of field-glasses and his finger on a button which worked a buzzer under the third-base coaching box. The coacher tipped the batter off what was coming and the signal-stealing device had worked perfectly. The hitters had all waited for the high fast ones in those days, as they can be hit easier if a man knows that they are coming and can also be hit farther.

Ed Delahanty, Philadelphia Phillies

But, after the buzzer had been discovered and the delivery of pitchers could not be accurately forecast, this ability to hit high fast ones vanished, but not the tradition. The result was that this Philadelphia club was getting a steady diet of curves and hitting them hard, not expecting anything else.

When I first pitched against Delahanty, his reputation as a hitter gave him a big edge on me. Therefore, I was willing to take any kind of advice calculated to help me, but eventually I had to find out for myself. If I had taken a chance on mixing them up the first time he faced me, I still doubt if he would have made those two long hits, but it was his reputation working in my mind and the idea that he ate up high fast balls that prevented me from taking the risk.

Each pitcher has to find out for himself what a man is going to hit. It's all right to take advice at first, but, if this does not prove to be the proper prescription, it's up to him to experiment and not continue to feed him the sort of balls that he is hitting.

Reputations count for a great deal in the Big-Leagues. Cobb has a record as being a great base runner, and I believe that he steals ten bases a season on this reputation. The catcher knows he is on the bag, realizes that he is going to steal, fears him, hurries his throw, and, in his anxiety, it goes bad. Cobb is safe, whereas, if he had been an ordinary runner with no reputation, he would probably have been thrown out. Pitchers who have made names for themselves in the Big-Leagues, have a much easier time winning as a consequence.

"Ty" Cobb, Detroit Tigers

"All he's got to do is to throw his glove into the box to beat that club," is an old expression in baseball, which means that the opposing batters fear the pitcher and that his reputation will carry him through if he has nothing whatever on the ball.

Newspapers work on the mental attitude of Big-League players. This has been most marked in Cincinnati, and I believe that the local newspapers have done as much as anything to keep a pennant away from that town. When the team went south for the spring practice, the newspapers printed glowing reports of the possibilities of the club winning the pennant, but, when the club started to fall down in the race, they would knock the men, and it would take the heart out of the players.

Almost enough good players have been let go by the Cincinnati team to make a world's championship club. There are Donlin, Seymour, Steinfeldt, Lobert and many more. Ball players inhale the accounts printed in the newspapers, and a correspondent with a grouch has ruined the prospects of many a good player and club. The New York newspapers, first by the great amount of publicity given to his old record, and then by criticizing him for not making a better showing, had a great deal to do with Marquard failing to make good the first two years he was in New York, as I have shown.

A smart manager in the Big-League is always working to keep his valuable stars in the right frame of mind. On the last western trip, the Giants made in the season of 1911, when they won the pennant by taking eighteen games out of twenty-two games, McGraw refused to permit any of the men to play cards. He realized that often the stakes ran high and that the losers brooded over the money which they lost and were thinking of this rather than the game when on the ball field. It hurt their playing, so there were no cards. He also carried "Charley" Faust, the Kansas Jinx killer, along to keep the players amused and because it was thought that he was good luck. It helped their mental attitude.

The treatment of a new player when he first arrives is different now from what it was in the old days. Once there was a time when the veteran looked upon the recruit with suspicion and the feeling that he had come to take his job and his bread and butter from him. If a young pitcher was put into the box, the old catcher would do all that he could to irritate him, and many times he would inform the batters of the other side what he was going to throw.

"He's tryin' to horn my friend Bill out of a job," I have heard catchers charge against a youngster.

This attitude drove many a star ball player back to the minors because he couldn't make good under the adverse circumstances, but nothing of the sort exists now. Each veteran does all that he can to help the youngster, realizing that on the younger generation depends the success of the club, and that no one makes any money by being on a loser. Travelling with a tail-end ball club is the poorest pastime in the world. I would rather ride in the first coach of a funeral procession.

The youngster is treated more courteously now when he first arrives. In the old days, the veterans of the club sized up the recruit and treated him like a stranger for days, which made him feel as if he were among enemies instead of friends, and, as a result, it was much harder for him to make good. Now all hands make him a companion from the start unless he shows signs of being unusually fresh.

There is a lot to baseball in the Big-Leagues besides playing the game. No man can have a "yellow streak" and last. He must not pay much attention to his nerves or temperament. He must hide every flaw. It's all part of the psychology of baseball. But the saddest words of all to a pitcher are three—"Take Him Out."

# Pitching in a Pinch

*Many Pitchers Are Effective in a Big-League Ball Game until that Heart-Breaking Moment Arrives Known as the "Pinch"—It Is then that the Man in the Box is Put to the Severest Test by the Coachers and the Players on the Bench—Victory or Defeat Hangs on his Work in that Inning—Famous "Pinches."*

**IN MOST** Big-League ball games, there comes an inning on which hangs victory or defeat. Certain intellectual fans call it the crisis; college professors, interested in the sport, have named it the psychological moment; Big-League managers mention it as the "break," and pitchers speak of the "pinch."

This is the time when each team is straining every nerve either to win or to prevent defeat. The players and spectators realize that the outcome of the inning is of vital importance. And in most of these pinches, the real burden falls on the pitcher. It is at this moment that he is "putting all he has" on the ball, and simultaneously his opponents are doing everything they can to disconcert him.

Managers wait for this break, and the shrewd league leader can often time it. Frequently a certain style of play is adopted to lead up to the pinch, then suddenly a slovenly mode of attack is changed, and the team comes on with a rush in an effort to break up the game. That is the real test of a pitcher. He must be able to live through these squalls.

Two evenly matched clubs have been playing through six innings with neither team gaining any advantage. Let us say that they are the Giants and the Chicago Cubs.

Suddenly the Chicago pitcher begins to weaken in the seventh. Spectators cannot perceive this, but McGraw, the Giants' manager, has detected some crack. All has been quiet on the bench up to this moment. Now the men begin to fling about sweaters and move around, one going to the water cooler to get a drink, another picking up a bat or two and flinging them in the air, while four or five prospective hitters are lined up, swinging several sticks apiece, as if absolutely confident that each will get his turn at the plate.

The two coaches on the side lines have become dancing dervishes, waving sweaters and arms wildly, and shouting various words of discouragement to the pitcher which are calculated to make his job as soft as a bed of concrete. He has pitched three balls to the batter, and McGraw vehemently protests to the umpire that the twirler is not keeping his foot on the slab. The game is delayed while this is discussed at the pitcher's box and the umpire brushes off the rubber strip with a whisk broom.

There is a kick against these tactics from the other bench, but the damage has been done. The pitcher passes the batter, forgets what he ought to throw to the next man, and cannot get the ball where he wants it. A base hit follows. Then he is gone. The following batter triples, and, before another pitcher can be warmed up, three or four runs are across the plate, and the game is won. That explains why so many wise managers keep a pitcher warming up when the man in the box is going strong.

It is in the pinch that the pitcher shows whether or not he is a Big-Leaguer. He must have something besides curves then. He needs a head, and he has to use it. It is the acid test. That is the reason so many men, who shine in the minor leagues, fail to make good in the majors. They cannot stand the fire.

A young pitcher came to the Giants a few years ago. I won't mention his name because he has been pitching good minor-league ball since. He was a wonder with the bases empty but let a man or two get on the sacks, and he wouldn't know whether he was in a pitcher's box or learning aviation in the Wright school, and he acted a lot more like an aviator in the crisis. McGraw looked him over twice.

"He's got a spine like a charlotte russe," declared "Mac," after his second peek, and he passed him back to the bushes.

Several other Big-League managers, tempted by this man's brilliant record in the minors, have tried him out since, but he has always gone back. McGraw's judgment of the man was correct.

On the other hand, Otis Crandall came to the New York club a few years ago a raw country boy from Indiana. I shall never forget how he looked the first spring I saw him in Texas. The club had a large number of recruits and was short of uniforms. He was among the last of the hopefuls to arrive and there was no suit for him, so, in a pair of regular trousers with his coat off, he began chasing flies in the outfield. His head hung down on his chest, and, when not playing, a cigarette drooped out of the corner of his mouth. But he turned out to be a very good fly chaser, and McGraw admired his persistency.

"What are you?" McGraw asked him one day.

"A pitcher," replied Crandall. Two words constitute an oration for him.

"Let's see what you've got," said McGraw.

Crandall warmed up, and he didn't have much of anything besides a sweeping outcurve and a good deal of speed. He looked less like a pitcher than

Otis Crandall, New York Giants

any of the spring crop, but McGraw saw something in him and kept him. The result is he has turned out to be one of the most valuable men on the club, because he is there in a pinch. He couldn't be disturbed if the McNamaras tied a bomb to him, with a time fuse on it set for "at once." He is the sort of pitcher who is best

when things look darkest. I've heard the crowd yelling, when he has been pitching on the enemy's ground, so that a sixteen-inch gun couldn't have been heard if it had gone off in the lot.
"That crowd was making some noise," I've said to Crandall after the inning.

"Was it?" asked Otie. "I didn't notice it."

One day in 1911, he started a game in Philadelphia and three men got on the bases with no one out, along about the fourth or fifth inning. He shut them out without a run. It was the first game he had started for a long while, his specialty having been to enter a contest, after some other pitcher had gotten into trouble, with two or three men on the bases and scarcely any one out. After he came to the bench with the threatening inning behind him, he said to me:

"Matty, I didn't feel at home out there to-day until a lot of people got on the bases. I'll be all right now."

And he was. I believe that Crandall is the best pitcher in a pinch in the National League and one of the most valuable men to a team, for he can play any position and bats hard. Besides being a great pinch pitcher, he can also hit in a crush, and won many games for the Giants in 1911 that way.

Very often spectators think that a pitcher has lost his grip in a pinch, when really he is playing inside baseball. A game with Chicago in Chicago back in 1908 (not the famous contest that cost the Giants a championship; I did not have any grip at all that day; but one earlier in the season) best illustrates the point I want to bring out. Mordecai Brown and I were having a pitchers' duel, and the Giants were in the lead by the score of 1 to 0 when the team took the field for the ninth inning.

It was one of those fragile games in which one run makes a lot of difference, the sort that has a fringe of nervous prostration for the spectators. Chance was up first in the ninth and he pushed a base hit to right field. Steinfeldt followed with a triple that brought Chance home and left the run which would win the game for the Cubs on third base. The crowd was shouting like mad, thinking I was done. I looked at the hitters, waiting to come up, and saw Hofman and Tinker swinging their bats in anticipation. Both are dangerous men, but the silver lining was my second look, which revealed to me Kling and Brown following Hofman and Tinker.

Without a second's hesitation, I decided to pass both Hofman and Tinker, because the run on third base would win the game anyway if it scored, and with three men on the bags instead of one, there would be a remote chance for a triple play, besides making a force out at the plate possible. Remember that no one was out at this time. Kling and Brown had always been easy for me.

When I got two balls on Hofman, trying to make him hit at a bad one, the throng stood up in the stand and tore splinters out of the floor with its feet. And then I passed Hofman. The spectators misunderstood my motive.

"He's done. He's all in," shouted one man in a voice which was one of the carrying, persistent, penetrating sort. The crowd took the cry up and stamped its feet and cheered wildly.

Solly Hofman, Chicago Cubs

Then I passed Tinker, a man, as I have said before, who has had a habit of making trouble for me. The crowd quieted down somewhat, perhaps because it was not possible for it to cheer any louder, but probably because the spectators thought that now it would be only a matter of how many the Cubs would win by. The bases were full, and no one was out.

But that wildly cheering crowd had worked me up to greater effort, and I struck Kling out and then Brown followed him back to the bench for the same reason. Just one batter stood between me and a tied score now. He was John Evers, and the crowd having lost its chortle of victory, was begging him to make the hit which would bring just one run over the plate. They were surprised by my recuperation after having passed two men. Evers lifted a gentle fly to left field and the three men were left on the bases. The Giants eventually won that game in the eleventh inning by the score of 4 to 1.

But that system doesn't always work. Often, I have passed a man to get a supposedly poor batter up and then had him bang out a base hit. My first successful year in the National League was 1901, although I joined the Giants in the middle of the season of 1900. The Boston club at that time had a pitcher named "Kid" Nichols who was a great twirler. The first two games I pitched against the Boston club were against this man, and I won the first in Boston and the second in New York, the latter by the score of 2 to 1.

Both teams then went west for a three weeks'

"Kid" Nichols, Boston Nationals

trip, and when the Giants returned a series was scheduled with Boston at the Polo Grounds. There was a good deal of speculation as to whether I would again beat the veteran "Kid" Nichols, and the newspapers, discussing the promised pitching duel, stirred up considerable enthusiasm over it. Of course, I, the youngster, was eager to make it three straight over the veteran. Neither team had scored at the beginning of the eighth inning. Boston runners got on second and third bases with two out, and Fred Tenney, then playing first base on the Boston club, was up at the bat. He had been hitting me hard that day, and I decided to pass him and take a chance on "Dick" Cooley, the next man, and a weak batter. So Tenney got his base on balls, and the sacks were full.

Two strikes were gathered on Cooley, one at which he swung and the other called, and I was beginning to congratulate myself on my excellent judgment, which was really counting my chickens while they were still in the incubator. I attempted to slip a fast one over on Cooley and got the ball a little too high. The result was that he stepped into it and made a three base hit which eventually won the game by the score of 3 to 0. That was once when passing a man to get a weak batter did not work.

"Dick" Cooley, Boston Nationals

I have always been against a twirler pitching himself out, when there is no necessity for it, as so many youngsters do. They burn them through for eight innings and then, when the pinch comes, something is lacking. A pitcher must remember that there are eight other men in the game, drawing more or less salary to stop balls hit at them, and he must have confidence in them. Some pitchers will put all that they have on each ball. This is foolish for two reasons.

In the first place, it exhausts the man physically and, when the pinch comes, he has not the strength to last it out. But second and more important, it shows the batters everything that he has, which is senseless. A man should always hold something in reserve, a surprise to spring when things get tight. If a pitcher has displayed his whole assortment to the batters in the early part of the game and has used all his speed and his fastest breaking curve, then, when the crisis comes, he "hasn't anything" to fall back on.

Like all youngsters, I was eager to make a record during my first year in the Big-League, and in one of the first games I pitched against Cincinnati I made the mistake of putting all that I had on every ball. We were playing at the Polo Grounds, and the Giants had the visitors beaten 2 to 0, going into the last inning. I had been popping them through, trying to strike out every hitter and had not held anything in reserve. The first man to the bat in the ninth got a single, the next a two bagger, and by the time they had stopped hitting me, the scorer had credited the Cincinnati club with four runs, and we lost the game, 4 to 2.

I was very much down in the mouth over the defeat, after I had the game apparently won, and George Davis, then the manager of the Giants, noticed it in the clubhouse. "Never mind, Matty," he said, "it was worth it. The game ought to teach you not to pitch your head off when you don't need to."

It did. I have never forgotten that lesson. Many spectators wonder why a pitcher does not work as hard as he can all through the game, instead of just in the pinches. If he did, they argue, there would be no pinches. But there would be, and, if the pitcher did not conserve his energy, the pinches would usually go against him.

Sometimes bawling at a man in a pinch has the opposite effect from that desired. Clark Griffith, recently of Cincinnati, has a reputation in the Big-Leagues for being a bad man to upset a pitcher from the coacher's box. Off the field he is one of the decentest fellows in the game, but, when talking to a pitcher, he is very irritating. I was working in a game against the Reds in Cincinnati one day, just after he had been made manager of the club, and Griffith spent the afternoon and a lot of breath trying to get me going. The Giants were ahead, 5 to 1, at the beginning of the seventh. In the Cincinnati half of that inning, "Mike" Mitchell tripled with the bases full and later tallied on an outfield fly which tied the score. The effect this had on Griffith was much the same as that of a lighted match on gasoline.

"Now, you big blond," he shouted at me, "we've got you at last."

I expected McGraw to take me out, as it looked in that inning as if I was not right, but he did not, and I pitched along up to the ninth with the score still tied and with Griffith, the carping critic, on the side lines. We failed to count in our half, but the first Cincinnati batter got on the bases, stole second, and went to third on a sacrifice. He was there with one out.

Clark Griffith, Cincinnati Reds

"Here's where we get you," chortled Griffith. "This is the point at which you receive a terrible showing up."

I tried to get the next batter to hit at bad balls, and he refused, so that I lost him. I was afraid to lay the ball over the plate in this crisis, as a hit or an outfield fly meant the game. Hoblitzell and Mitchell, two of Griffith's heaviest batters, were scheduled to arrive at the plate next.

"You ought to be up, Mike," yelled the Cincinnati manager at Mitchell, who was swinging a couple of sticks preparatory to his turn at the bat. "Too bad you won't get a lick, old man, because Hobby's going to break it up right here."

Something he said irritated me, but instead of worrying me, it made me feel more like pitching. I seldom talk to a coacher, but I turned to Griffith and said:

"I'll bring Mike up, and we'll see what he can do."
I deliberately passed Hoblitzell without even giving him a chance to hit at a single ball. It wasn't to make a grandstand play I did this, but because it was baseball.

One run would win the game anyway, and, with more men on the bases, there were more plays possible. Besides Hoblitzell is a nasty hitter, and I thought that I had a better chance of making Mitchell hit the ball on the ground, a desirable thing under the conditions.

Mike Mitchell, Cincinnati Reds

"Now, Mike," urged Griffith, as Mitchell stepped up to the plate, "go as far as you like. Blot up the bases, old boy. This blond is gone."

That sort of talk never bothers me. I had better luck with Mitchell than I had hoped. He struck out. The next batter was easy, and the Giants won the game in the tenth inning. According to the newspaper reports, I won twenty-one or twenty-two games before Cincinnati beat me again, so it can be seen that joshing in pinches is not effective against all pitchers. A manager must judge the temperament of his victim. But Griffith has never stopped trying to rag me. In 1911, when the Giants were west on their final trip, I was warming up in Cincinnati before a game, and he was batting out flies near me. He would talk to me between each ball he hit to the outfield.

"Got anything to-day, Matty?" he asked. "Guess there ain't many games left in you. You're getting old."

When I broke into the National League, the Brooklyn club had as bad a bunch of men to bother a pitcher as I ever faced. The team had won the championship in 1900, and naturally they were all pretty chesty. When I first began to play in 1901, this crowd—Kelly, Jennings, Keeler and Hanlon—got after me pretty strong. But I seemed to get pitching nourishment out of their line of conversation and won a lot of games.

At last, so I have been told, Hanlon, who was the manager, said to his conversational ball players:

"Lay off that Mathewson kid. Leave him alone. He likes the chatter you fellows spill out there." They did not bother me after that, but this bunch spoiled many a promising young pitcher.

Speaking of sizing up the temperament of batters and pitchers in a pinch, few persons realize that it was a little bit of carelessly placed conversation belonging to "Chief" Bender, the Indian pitcher on the Athletics, that did as much as anything to give the Giants the first game in the 1911 world's series.

"Josh" Devore, the left-fielder on the New York team, is an in-and-out batter, but he is a bulldog in a pinch and is more apt to make a hit in a tight place than when the bases are empty. And he is quite as likely to strike out. He is the type of ball player who cannot be rattled. With "Chief" Myers on second base, the score tied, and two out, Devore came to the bat in the seventh inning of the first game.

"Chief" Meyers, New York Giants

"Look at little 'Josh,'" said Bender, who had been talking to batters all through the game.

Devore promptly got himself into the hole with two strikes and two balls on him, but a little drawback like that never worries "Josh."

"I'm going to pitch you a curved ball over the outside corner," shouted Bender as he wound up.

"I know it, Chief," replied "Josh," and he set himself to receive just that sort of delivery.

Up came the predicted curve over the outside corner. "Josh" hit it to left field for two bases and brought home the winning run. Bender evidently thought that, by telling Devore what he was actually going to pitch, he would make him think he was going to cross him.

"I knew it would be a curve ball," Devore told me after the game. "With two and two, he would be crazy to hand me anything else. When he made that crack, I guessed that he was trying to cross me by telling the truth. Before he spoke, I wasn't sure which corner he was going to put it over, but he tipped me."

Some batters might have been fooled by those tactics. It was taking a chance in a pinch, and Bender lost.

Very few of the fans who saw this first game of the 1911 world's series realize that the "break" in that contest came in the fifth inning. The score was tied, with runners on second and third bases with two out, when "Eddie" Collins, the fast second baseman of the Athletics, and a dangerous hitter, came to the bat. I realized that I was skating on thin ice and was putting everything I had on the ball. Collins hit a slow one down the first base line, about six feet inside the bag.

With the hit, I ran over to cover the base, and Merkle made for the ball, but he had to get directly in my line of approach to field it. Collins, steaming down the base line, realized that, if he could get the decision at first on this hit, his team would probably win the game, as the two other runners could score easily. In a flash, I was aware of this, too.

"I'll take it," yelled Merkle, as he stopped to pick up the ball.

Seeing Merkle and me in front of him, both heavy men, Collins knew that he could not get past us standing up. When still ten or twelve feet from the bag, he slid, hoping to take us unawares and thus avoid being touched. He could then scramble to the bag. As soon as he jumped, I realized what he hoped to do, and, fearing that Merkle would miss him, I grabbed the first baseman and hurled him at Collins. It was an old-fashioned, football shove, Merkle landing on Collins and touching him out. A great many of the spectators believed that I had interfered with Merkle on the play. As a matter of fact, I thought that it was the crisis of the game and knew that, if Collins was not put out, we would probably lose. That football shove was a brand-new play to me in baseball, invented on the spur of the second, but it worked.

Eddie Collins, Philadelphia Athletics

In minor leagues, there are fewer games in which a "break" comes. It does not develop in all Big-League contests by any means. Sometimes one team starts to win in the first inning and simply runs away from the other club all the way. But in all close games the pinch shows up.

It happens in many contests in the major leagues because of the almost perfect baseball played. Depending on his fielders, a manager can play for this "break." And when the pinch comes, it is a case of the batter's nerve against the pitcher's.

# Big-League Pitchers and Their Peculiarities.

*Nearly Every Pitcher in the Big-Leagues Has Some Temperamental or Mechanical Flaw which he is Constantly Trying to Hide, and which Opposing Batters are always Endeavoring to Uncover—The Giants Drove Coveleski, the Man who Beat them out of a Pennant, Back to the Minor Leagues by Taunting him on One Sore Point—Weaknesses of Other Stars.*

**LIKE GREAT** artists in other fields of endeavor, many Big-League pitchers are temperamental. "Bugs" Raymond, "Rube" Waddell, "Slim" Sallee, and "Wild Bill" Donovan are ready examples of the temperamental type. The first three are the sort of men of whom the manager is never sure. He does not know, when they come into the ballpark, whether or not they are in condition to work. They always carry with them a delightful atmosphere of uncertainty.

"Wild" Bill Donovan, Detroit Tigers

In contrast to this eccentric group, there are those with certain mechanical defects in their pitching of which opposing clubs take advantage. Last comes the irritable, nervous box artist who must have things just so, even down to the temperature, before he can work satisfactorily.

"As delicate as prima donnas," says John McGraw of this variety.

He speaks of the man who loses his love for his art when his shirt is too tight, or a toe is sore. This style, perhaps, is the most difficult for a manager to handle, unless it is the uncertain, eccentric sort.

As soon as a new pitcher breaks into the Big-Leagues, seven clubs are studying him with microscopic care to discover some flaw in his physical style or a temperamental weakness on which his opponents can play. Naturally, if the man has such a "groove," his teammates are endeavoring to hide it, but it soon leaks out and becomes general gossip around the circuit. Then the seven clubs start aiming at this flaw, and oftentimes the result is that a promising young pitcher, because he has some one definite weakness, goes back to the minors. A crack in the temperament is the worst. Mechanical defects can usually be remedied when discovered.

Few baseball fans know that the Giants drove a man back to the minor leagues who once pitched them out of a pennant. The club was tipped off to a certain, unfortunate circumstance in the twirler's early life which left a lasting impression on his mind. The players never let him forget this when he was in a game, and it was like constantly hitting him on a boil.

Coveleski won three games for the Philadelphia National League club from the Giants back in 1908, when one of these contests would have meant a pennant to the New York club and possibly a world's championship. That was the season the fight was decided in a single game with the Chicago Cubs after the regular schedule had been played out. Coveleski was hailed as a wonder for his performance.

Just after the season closed, "Tacks" Ashenbach, the scout for the Cincinnati club, now dead, and formerly a manager in the league where Coveleski got his start, came to McGraw and laughed behind his hand.

"Mac," he said, "I'm surprised you let that big Pole beat you out of a championship. I can give you the prescription to use every time that he starts working. All you have to do is to imitate a snare drum."

"What are you trying to do—kid me?" asked McGraw, for he was still tolerably irritable over the outcome of the season.

"Try it," was Ashenbach's laconic reply.

The result was that the first game Coveleski started against the Giants the next season, there was a chorus of "rat-a-tat-tats" from the bench, with each of the coaches doing a "rat-a-tat-tat" solo, for we decided, after due consideration, this was the way to imitate a snare drum. We would have tried to imitate a calliope if we had thought that it would have done any good against this pitcher.

"I'll hire a fife and drum corps if the tip is worth anything," declared McGraw.

"Rat-a-tat-tat! Rat-a-tat-tat!" came the chorus as Coveleski wound up to pitch the first ball. It went wide of the plate.

Harry Covelseki, Philadelphia Phillies

"Rat-a-tat-tat! Rat-a-tat-tat!" it was repeated all through the inning. When Coveleski walked to the Philadelphia bench at the end of the first round, after the Giants had made three runs off him, he looked over at us and shouted:

"You think you're smart, don't you?"

"Rat-a-tat-tat! Rat-a-tat-tat!" was the only reply.

But now we knew we had him. When a pitcher starts to talk back, it is a cinch that he is irritated. So, the deadly chorus was kept up in volleys, until the umpire stopped us, and then it had to be in a broken fire, but always there was the "Rat-a-tat-tat! Rat-a-tat-tat!" When Coveleski looked at McGraw coaching on third base, the manager made as if to beat a snare drum, and as he glanced at Latham stationed at first, "Arlie" would reply with the "rat-a-tat-tat."

The team on the bench sounded like a fife and drum corps without the fifes, and Coveleski got no peace. In the fourth inning, after the game had been hopelessly lost by the Philadelphia club, Coveleski was taken out. We did not understand the reason for it, but we all knew that we had found Coveleski's "groove" with that "rat-a-tat-tat" chorus. The man who had beaten the New York club out of a pennant never won another game against the Giants.

"Say," said McGraw to "Tacks" Ashenbach the next time the club was in Cincinnati, "there are two things I want to ask you. First, why does that 'rat-a-tat-tat' thing get under Coveleski's skin so badly, and second, why didn't you mention it to us when he was beating the club out of a championship last fall?"

"Never thought of it," asserted Ashenbach. "Just chanced to be telling stories one day last winter about the old times in the Tri-State, when that weakness of Coveleski's happened to pop into my mind. Thought maybe he was cured."

"Cured!" echoed McGraw. "Only way he could be cured of that is to poison him. But tip me. Why is it?"

"Well, this is the way I heard it," answered Ashenbach. "When he was a coal miner back in Shamokin, Pennsylvania, he got stuck on some Jane who was very fond of music. Everybody who was anyone played in the Silver Cornet Band down in Melodeon Hall on Thursday nights. The girl told Coveleski that she couldn't see him with an X-ray unless he broke into the band.

"'But I can't play any instrument,' said the Pole.

"'Well, get busy and learn, and don't show around here until you have,' answered the girl."

Now Coveleski had no talent for music, so he picked out the snare drum as his victim and started practicing regularly, getting some instruction from the local bandmaster. After he had driven all the neighbors pretty nearly crazy, the bandmaster said he would give him a show at the big annual concert, when he tried to get all the pieces in his outfit that he could. Things went all right until it was time for Coveleski to come along with a little bit on the snare drum, and then he was nowhere in the neighborhood. He didn't even swing at it. But later, when the leader waved for a solo from the fiddle, Coveleski mistook it for his hit-and-run sign and came in so strong on the snare drum that no one could identify the fiddle in the mix-up.

"The result was that the leader asked for waivers on old Coveleski very promptly, and the girl was not long in following suit. That snare drum incident has been the sore point in his makeup ever since."

"I wish I'd known it last fall about the first of September," declared McGraw.

But the real snapper came later when the Cincinnati club was whipsawed on the information. In a trade with Philadelphia, Griffith got Coveleski for Cincinnati along with several other players. Each game he started against us he got the old "rat-a-tat-tat." Griffith protested to the umpires, but it is impossible to stop a thing of that sort even though the judges of play did try.

The Pole did not finish another game against the Giants until his last in the Big-League. One day we were hitting him near and far, and the "rat-a-tat-tat" chorus was only interrupted by the rattle of the bats against the ball, when he looked in at the bench to see if Griffith wanted to take him out, for it was about his usual leaving time.

"Stay in there and get it," shouted back Griff.

Coveleski did. He absorbed nineteen hits and seventeen runs at the hands of the Giants, this man who had taken a championship of the National League away from us.

That night Griffith asked for waivers on him, and he left the Big-Leagues for good. He was a good twirler, except for that one flaw, which cost him his place in the big show. There is little mercy among professional ball players when a game is at stake, especially if the man has taken a championship away from a team by insisting upon working out of his turn, so he can win games that will benefit his club not a scintilla.

Mordecai Brown, the great pitcher of the Chicago Cubs and the man who did more than any other one player to bring four National League pennants and two world's championships to that club, has a physical deformity which has turned out to be an advantage. Many years ago, Brown lost most of the first finger of his right hand in an argument with a feed cutter, said finger being amputated at the second joint; while his third finger is shorter than it should be, because a hot grounder carried part of it away one day. In some strange way, Brown has achieved wonders with this crippled hand. It is on account of the missing finger that he is called "Three Fingered" Brown,

Mordecai Brown, Chicago Cubs

and he is better known by that appellation than by his real name.

Brown beat the Giants a hard game one day in 1911, pitching against me. He had a big curve, lots of speed, and absolute control. The Giants could not touch him. Next day McGraw was out warming up with Arthur Wilson, the young catcher on the club.

"Wonder if he gets any new curve with that short first finger?" said McGraw, and thereupon crooked his own initial digit and began trying to throw the ball in different ways off it to see what the result would be. Finally, he decided:

"No, I guess he doesn't get anything extra with the abbreviated finger, but that's lucky for you fellows, because, if I thought he did, I'd have a surgeon out here to-morrow operating on the first fingers of each of you pitchers."

Brown is my idea of the almost perfect pitcher He is always ready to work. It is customary for most managers in the Big-Leagues to say to a man on the day he is slated to pitch: "Well, how do you feel to-day? Want to work?" Then if the twirler is not right, he has a chance to say so.

But Brown always replies: "Yes, I'm ready."

He likes to pitch and is in chronic condition. It will usually be found at the end of a season that he has taken part in more games than any other pitcher in the country. He held the Chicago pitching staff together in 1911.

"Three Fingered" Brown is a finished pitcher in all departments of the game. Besides being a great worker, he is a wonderful fielder and sure death on bunts. He spends weeks in the spring preparing himself to field short hits in the infield, and it is fatal to try to bunt against him. He has perfected and used successfully for three years a play invented by "Joe" McGinnity, the former Giant pitcher.

"Joe" McGinnity, New York Giants

This play is with men on first and second bases and no one out or one out. The batter tries to sacrifice, but instead of fielding the ball to first base, which would advance the two base runners as intended, Brown makes the play to third and thus forces out the man nearest the plate. This is usually successful unless the bunt is laid down perfectly along the first base line, so that the ball cannot be thrown to third base.

The Cubs have always claimed it was this play which broke the Detroit club's heart in the world's series in 1908, and turned the tide so that the Cubs took the championship. The American League team was leading in the first game, and runners were on first and second bases, "Ty" Cobb being on the middle sack. It was evident that the batter would try to sacrifice. Brown walked over to Steinfeldt, playing third base, pulling out a chew of tobacco as he went.

"No matter what this guy does or where he hits it, stick to your bag," ordered Brown.

Then he put the chew of tobacco in his mouth, a sign which augurs ill for his opponents, and pitched a low one to the batter, a perfect ball to bunt. He followed the pitch through and was on top of the plate as the batter laid it down. The ball rolled slowly down the third base line until Brown pounced on it. He whirled and drove the ball at Steinfeldt, getting Cobb by a foot. That play carried Detroit off its feet, as a sudden reversal often will a ball club, when things are apparently breaking for it. Cobb, the Tigers' speed flash, had been caught at third base on an attempted sacrifice, an unheard of play, and, from that point on, the American Leaguers wilted, according to the stories of Chance and his men.

It is Brown's perfect control that has permitted catchers like Kling and Archer to make such great records as throwers. This pitcher can afford to waste a ball—that is, pitch out so the batter cannot hit it, but putting the catcher in a perfect position to throw—

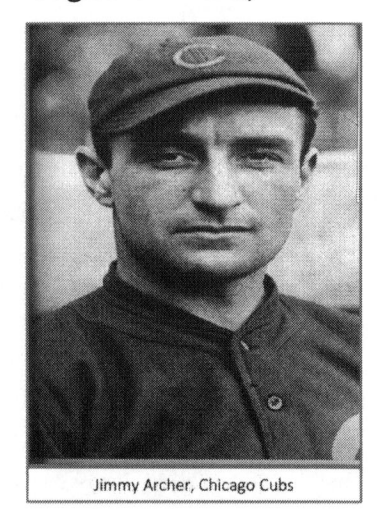

Jimmy Archer, Chicago Cubs

and then he knows he can get the next one over. A catcher's efficiency as a thrower depends largely on the pitcher's ability to have good enough control of the ball to be able to pitch out when it is necessary. Brown helps a catcher by the way in which he watches the bases, not permitting the runners to take any lead on him. All around, I think that he is one of the most finished pitchers of the game.

Russell Ford, of the New York American League club, has a hard pitching motion because he seems to throw a spit ball with a jerk. He cannot pitch more than one good game in four or five days. McGraw had detected this weakness from watching the Highlanders play before the post-season series in 1910 and took advantage of it.

Russell Ford, New York Highlanders

"If Ford pitches to-day," said McGraw to his team in the clubhouse before the first game, "wait everything out to the last minute. Make him pitch every ball you can."

McGraw knew that the strain on Ford's arm would get him along toward the end of the game. In the eighth inning the score was tied when Devore came to the bat. No crack in Ford was perceptible to the rest of us, but

McGraw must have detected some slight sign of weakening.

He stopped "Josh" on the way to the plate and ordered: "Now go ahead and get him."

By the time the inning was over, the Giants had made four runs, and eventually won the game by the score of 5 to 1. McGraw just played for this flaw in Ford's pitching and hung his whole plan of battle on the chance of it showing.

"Old Cy" Young has the absolutely perfect pitching motion. When he jumped from the National League to the Boston American League club some years ago, during the war times, many National League players thought that he was through.

"Cy" Young, Boston Americans

"What," said Fred Clarke, the manager of the Pittsburg club, "you American Leaguers letting that old boy make good in your set? Why, he was done when he jumped the National. He'd lost his speed."

"But you ought to see his curve ball," answered "Bill" Dineen, then pitching for the Boston Americans.

"Curve ball," echoed Clarke.

"He never had any curve that it didn't take a microscope to find. He depended on his speed." "Well, he's got one now," replied Dineen.

Clarke had a chance to look at the curve ball later, for, with Dineen, Young did a lot toward winning the world's championship for Boston from Pittsburg in 1903. The old pitcher was wise enough to realize, when he began to lose his speed, that he would have to develop a curve ball or go back to the minors, and he set to work and produced a peach. He is still pitching—for the National League now—and he will win a lot of games yet.

When he came back in 1911, the American Leaguers said: "What, going to let that old man in your show again? He's done."

Maybe he will yet figure in another world's championship. One never can tell. Anyway, he has taken a couple of falls out of Pittsburg just for good luck since he came back to the National League.

Some pitchers depend largely on their motions to fool batters. "Motion pitchers" they might be called. Such an elaborate wind-up is developed that it is hard for a hitter to tell when and from where the ball is coming. "Slim" Sallee of the St. Louis Nationals hasn't any curve to mention, and he lacks speed, but he wins a lot of ball games on his motion.

"It's a crime," says McGraw, "to let a fellow like that beat you. Why, he has so little on the ball that it looks like one of those Salome dancers when it comes up to the plate, and actually makes me blush."

But Sallee will take a long wind-up and shoot one off his shoe tops and another from his shoulder while he is facing second base. He has good control, has catalogued the weaknesses of the batters, and can work the corners. With this capital, he was winning ball games for the Cardinals in 1911 until he fell off the water wagon. He is different from Raymond in that respect. When he is on the vehicle, he is on it, and, when he is off, he is distinctly a pedestrian.

The way the Giants try to beat Sallee is to get men on the bases, because then he has to cut down his motion or they will run wild on him. As soon as a runner gets on the bag with Sallee pitching, he tries to steal to make "Slim" reduce that long winding motion which is his greatest asset. But Sallee won several games from the Giants last season because we could not get enough men on the bases to beat him. He only gave us four or five hits per contest.

For a long time, "Josh" Devore, the Giants' left-fielder, was "plate shy" with left-handers—that is, he stepped away—and all the pitchers in the League soon learned of this and started shooting the first ball, a fast one, at his head to increase his natural timidity. Sallee, in particular, had him scared.

"Stand up there," said McGraw to "Josh" one day when Sallee was pitching, "and let him hit you. He hasn't speed enough to hurt you."

"Josh" did, got hit, and found out that what McGraw said was true. It cured him of being afraid of Sallee.

As getting men on the bases decreases Sallee's effectiveness, even if he is a left-hander, so it increases the efficiency of "Lefty" Leifield of Pittsburg. The Giants never regard Sallee as a left-hander with men on the bases. Most southpaws can keep a runner close to the bag because they are facing first base when in a position to pitch, but Sallee cannot. On the other hand, Leifield uses almost exactly the same motion to throw to first base as to pitch to the batter. These two

"Lefty" Leifield, Pittsburgh Pirates

are so nearly alike that he can change his mind after he starts and throw to the other place.

He keeps men hugging the bag, and it is next to impossible to steal bases on him. If he gets his arm so far forward in pitching to the batter that he cannot throw to the base, he can see a man start and pitchout, so the catcher has a fine chance to get the runner at second. If the signal is for a curved ball, he can make it a high curve, and the catcher is in position to throw.

Leifield has been working this combination pitch either to first base or the plate for years, and the motion for each is so similar that even the umpires cannot detect it and never call a balk on him.

A busher broke into the League with the Giants one fall and was batting against Pittsburg. There was a man on first base and Leifield started to pitch to the plate, saw by a quick glance that the runner was taking too large a lead, and threw to first. The youngster swung at the ball and started to run it out. Everyone laughed.

"What were you trying to do?" asked McGraw.

"I hit the ball," protested the bush leaguer.

That is how perfect Leifield's motion is with men on the bases. But most of his effectiveness resides in that crafty motion.

"Dummy" Taylor, New York Giants

Many New York fans will remember "Dummy" Taylor, the deaf and dumb pitcher of the Giants. He won ball games for the last two years he was with the club on his peculiar, whirling motion, but as soon as men got on the bases and he had to cut it down, McGraw would take him out. That swing and his irresistible good nature are still winning games in the International League, which used to be the Eastern.

So, if a pitcher expects to be a successful Big-Leaguer, he must guard against eccentricities of temperament and mechanical motion.

As I have said, Drucke of the Giants for a long time had a little movement with his foot which indicated to the runner when he was going to pitch, and they stole bases wildly on him. But McGraw soon discovered that something was wrong and corrected it.

The armor of a Big-Leaguer must be impenetrable, for there are seven clubs always looking for flaws in the manufacture, and "every little movement has a meaning of its own."

# Playing the Game from the Bench

*Behind Every Big-League Ball Game there Is a Master Mind which Directs the Moves of the Players—How McGraw Won Two Pennants for the Giants from the "Bench" and Lost One by Giving the Players Too Much Liberty—The Methods of "Connie" Mack and Other Great Leaders*

**THE BENCH!** To many fans who see a hundred Big-League ball games each season, this is a long, hooded structure from which the next batter emerges and where the players sit while their club is at bat. It is also the resort of the substitutes, manager, mascot and water cooler.

"Connie" Mack, Philadelphia Athletics

But to the ball player it is the headquarters. It is the place from which the orders come, and it is here that the battle is planned and from here the moves are executed. The manager sits here and pulls the wires, and his players obey him as if they were manikins.
"The batteries for to-day's game," says the umpire, "will be Sallee and Bresnahan for St. Louis; Wiltse and Meyers for New York."

"Bunt," says McGraw as his players scatter to take their positions on the field.

He repeats the order when they come to the bat for the first inning, because he knows that Sallee has two weaknesses, one being that he cannot field bunts and the other that a great deal of activity in the box tires him out so that he weakens. A bunting game hits at both these flaws.

As soon as Bresnahan observes the plan of battle, he arranges his players to meet the attack; draws in his third baseman, shifts the shortstop more down the line toward third base, and is on the alert himself to gather in slow rollers just in front of the plate. The idea is to give Sallee the minimum opportunity to get at the ball and reduce his fielding responsibilities to nothing or less. There is one thing about Sallee's style known to every Big-League manager. He is not half as effective with men on the bases, for he depends largely on his deceptive motion to fool the batters, and when he has to cut this down because runners are on the bases, his pitching ability evaporates.

After the old Polo Grounds had been burned down in the spring of 1911, we were playing St. Louis at American League Park one Saturday afternoon, and the final returns of the game were about 19 to 5 in our favor, as near as I can remember. We made thirteen runs in the first inning. Many spectators went away from the park talking about a slaughter and a runaway score and so on. That game was won in the very first inning when Sallee went into the box to pitch, and McGraw had murmured that mystic word "Bunt!"

The first batters bunted, bunted, bunted in monotonous succession. Sallee not yet in very good physical condition because it was early in the season, was stood upon his head by this form of attack. Bresnahan re-draped his infield to try to stop this onslaught, and then McGraw switched.

"Hit it," he directed the next batter.

A line drive whistled past Mowrey's ears, the man who plays third base on the Cardinals. He was coming in to get a bunt. Another followed. The break had come. Bresnahan removed Sallee and put another pitcher into the box, but once a ball club starts to hit the ball, it is like a

"Slim" Sallee, St. Louis Cardinals

skidding automobile. It can't be stopped. The Giants kept on and piled up a ridiculous and laughable score, which McGraw had made possible in the first inning by directing his men to bunt.

The Giants won the championship of the National League in 1904 and the New York fans gave the team credit for the victory. It was a club of young players, and McGraw realized this fact when he started his campaign. Every play that season was made from the bench, made by John McGraw through his agents, his manikins, who moved according to the wires which he pulled. And by the end of the summer his hands were badly calloused from pulling wires, but the Giants had the pennant.

When the batter was at the plate in a critical stage, he would stall and look to the "bench" for orders to discover whether to hit the ball out or lay it down, whether to try the hit and run, or wait for the base runner to attempt to steal. By stalling, I mean that he would tie his shoe or fix his belt or find any little excuse to delay the game so that he could get a flash at the "bench" for orders. A shoelace has played an important role in many a Big-League battle, as I will try to show later on in this story. If it ever became the custom to wear button shoes, the game would have to be revised.

As the batter looked toward the bench, McGraw might reach for his handkerchief to blow his nose, and the batter knew it was up to him to hit the ball out. Some days in that season of 1904 I saw McGraw blow his nose during a game until it was red and sore on the end, and then another day, when he had a cold in his head, he had to do without his handkerchief because he wanted to play a bunting game. Until his cold got better, he had to switch to another system of signs.

During that season, each coacher would keep his eye on the bench for orders. Around McGraw revolved the game of the Giants. He was the game. And most of that summer he spent upon the bench, because from there he could get the best look at the diamond, and his observations were not confined to one place or to one base runner. He was able to discover whether an outfielder was playing too close for a batter, or too far out, and rearrange the men. He could perhaps catch a sign from the opposing catcher and pass it along to the batter. And he won the pennant from the bench. He was seldom seen on the coaching lines that year.

Many fans wonder why, when the Giants get behind in a game, McGraw takes to the bench, after having been out on the coaching lines inning after inning while the club was holding its own or winning. Time and again I have heard him criticised for this by spectators and even by players on other clubs.

"McGraw is 'yellow,'" players have said to me. "Just as soon as his club gets behind, he runs for cover."

The crime of being "yellow" is the worst in the Big-Leagues. It means that a man is afraid, that he lacks the nerve to face the music. But McGraw and "yellow" are as far apart as the poles, or Alpha and Omega, or Fifth

Avenue and the Bowery, or any two widely separated and distant things. I have seen McGraw go on to ball fields where he is as welcome as a man with the black smallpox and face the crowd alone that, in the heat of its excitement, would like to tear him apart. I have seen him take all sorts of personal chances. He doesn't know what fear is, and in his bright lexicon of baseball there is no such word as "fear." His success is partly due to his indomitable courage.

There is a real reason for his going to the bench when the team gets behind. It is because this increases the club's chances of winning. From the bench he can see the whole field, can note where his fielders are playing, can get a peek at the other bench, and perhaps pick up a tip as to what to expect. He can watch his own pitcher or observe whether the opposing twirler drops his throwing arm as if weary. He is at the helm when "on the bench," and, noting any flaw in the opposition, he is in a position to take advantage of it at a moment's notice, or, catching some sign of faltering among his own men, he is immediately there to strengthen the weakness. Many a game he has pulled out of the fire by going back to the bench and watching. So, the idea obtained by many spectators that he is quitting is the wrong one. He is only fighting harder.

The Giants were playing Pittsburg one day in the season of 1909, and Clarke and McGraw had been having a great guessing match. It was one of those give-and-take games with plenty of batting, with one club forging ahead and then the other. Clarke had saved the game for Pittsburg in the sixth inning by a shoe-string. Leifield had been pitching up to this point, and he wasn't there or even in the neighborhood. But still the Pirates were leading by two runs, having previously knocked Ames out of the box. Doyle and McCormick made hits with no one out in our half of the sixth.

It looked like the "break," and McGraw was urging his players on to even up the score, when Clarke suddenly took off his sunglasses in left field and stooped down to tie his shoe. When he removes his sun-glasses that is a sign for a pitcher to warm up in a hurry, and "Babe" Adams sprinted to the outfield with a catcher and began to heat up. Clarke took all of five minutes to tie that shoe, McGraw violently protesting against the delay in the meantime. Fred Clarke has been known to wear out a pair of shoelaces in one game tying and untying them. After the shoe was fixed up, he jogged slowly to the bench and took Leifield out of the box. In the interim, Adams had had an opportunity to warm up, and Clarke raised his arm and ordered him into the box. He fanned the next two men, and the last batter hit an easy roller to Wagner. We were still two runs to the bad after that promising start in the sixth, and Clarke, for the time being, had saved the game by a shoestring.

McGraw, who had been on the coaching lines up to this point, retired to the bench after that, and I heard one of those wise spectators, sitting just behind our coop, who could tell Mr. Rockefeller how to run his business but who spends his life working as a clerk at $18 a week, remark to a friend: "It's all off now. McGraw has laid down."

Watching the game through eyes half shut and drawn to a focus, McGraw waited. In the seventh inning Clarke came to bat with two men on the bases. A hit would have won the game beyond any doubt. In a flash McGraw was on his feet and ran out to Meyers, catching. He stopped the game, and, with a wave of his arm, drew Harry McCormick, playing left field, in close to third base.

The game went on, and Wiltse twisted a slow curve over the outside corner of the plate to Clarke, a left-handed hitter. He timed his swing and sent a low hit singing over third base. McCormick dashed in and caught the ball off his shoe tops. That made three outs.

Harry McCormick, New York Giants

McGraw had saved our chances of victory right there, for had McCormick been playing where he originally intended before McGraw stopped the contest, the ball would have landed in unguarded territory and two runs would have been scored.

But McGraw had yet the game to win. As his team came to the bat for the seventh, he said:

"This fellow Adams is a youngster and liable to be nervous and wild. Wait."

The batters waited with the patience of Job. Each man let the first two balls pass him and made Adams pitch himself to the limit to every batter. It got on Adams's nerves. In the ninth he passed a couple of men, and a hit tied the score. Clarke left him in the box, for he was short of pitchers. On the game went to ten, eleven, twelve, thirteen, innings. The score was still tied and Wiltse was pitching like a machine. McGraw was on the bench, leaving the coaching to his lieutenants. The club was still waiting for the youngster to weaken.

At last, in the thirteenth, after one man had been put out, the eye of McGraw saw Adams drop his pitching arm to his side as if tired. It was only a minute motion. None of the spectators saw it, none of the players.

"Now hit it, boys," came the order from the "bench." The style was switched, and the game won when three hits were rattled out.

McGraw alone observed that sign of weakening and took advantage of it at the opportune time. He won the game from the bench.

That is what makes him a great manager, observing the little things. Anyone can see the big ones. If he had been on the coaching lines, he would not have had as good an opportunity to study the young pitcher, for he would have had to devote his attention to the base runners. He might have missed this sign of wilting.

McGraw is always studying a pitcher, particularly a new one in the League. The St. Louis club had a young pitcher last fall, named Laudermilk, who was being tried out. He had a brother on the team. In his first game against the Giants, played in St. Louis, he held us to a few scattered hits and gave us a terrific battle, only losing the game because one of his fielders made a costly error behind him.

The papers of St. Louis boosted him as another "Rube" Waddell. He was left-handed. McGraw laughed.
"All I want," he said, "is another crack at that Buttermilk after what I learned about him this afternoon. He can't control his curve, and all you fellows have got to do is wait for his fast one. He gave you that fight to-day because he had you all swinging at bad curve balls."

"Rube" Waddell, Philadelphia Athletics

Laudermilk made another appearance against the Giants later, and he made his disappearance in that game in the fourth inning, when only one was out to be exact, after we had scored five runs off him by waiting for his fast one, according to McGraw's orders.

After winning the pennant in 1904 by sitting on the bench, keeping away from the coaching lines, and making every play himself, McGraw decided that his men were older and knew the game and that he would give them more rein in 1905. He appeared oftener on the coaching lines and attended more to the base runners than to the game as a whole. But in the crises, he was the man who decided what was to be done. The club won the pennant that year and the world's championship. The players got very chesty immediately thereafter, and the buttons on their vests had to be shifted back to make room for the new measure. They knew the game and had won two pennants, besides a championship of the world.

So, in the season of 1906 McGraw started with a team of veterans, and it was predicted that he would repeat. But these men, who knew the game, were making decisions for themselves because McGraw was giving them more liberty. The runners went wild on the bases and tried things at the wrong stages.

They lost game after game. At last, after a particularly disastrous defeat one day, McGraw called his men together in the clubhouse and addressed them in this wise:

"Because you fellows have won two championships and beaten the Athletics is no reason for you all to believe that you are fit to write a book on how to play baseball. You are just running wild on the bases. You might as well not have a manager. Now don't anyone try to pull anything without orders. We will begin all over again."

But it is hard to teach old ballplayers new tricks, and several fines had to be imposed before the orders were obeyed. The club did not win the championship that year.

When McGraw won the pennant in 1911, he did it with a club of youngsters, many of them playing through their first whole season as regulars in the company. There were Snodgrass and Devore and Fletcher and Marquard. Every time a batter went to the plate, he had definite orders from the "bench" as to what he was to attempt—whether to take two, or lay the ball down, or swing, or work the hit and run. Each time that a man shot out from first base like a catapulted figure and slid into second, he had been ordered by McGraw to try to steal.

Art Fletcher, New York Giants

If players protested against his judgment, his invariable answer was:

"Do what I tell you, and I'll take the blame for mistakes." One of McGraw's laments is, "I wish I could be in three places at once."

I never heard him say it with such a ring to the words as after Snodgrass was touched out in the third game of the 1911 world's series, in the tenth inning, when his life might have meant victory in that game anyway. I have frequently referred to the incident in these stories, so most of my readers are familiar with the situation. Snodgrass was put out trying to get to third base on a short passed ball, after he had started back for second to recover some of the ground he had taken in too long a lead before the ball got to Lapp. McGraw's face took on an expression of agony as if he were watching his dearest friend die.

"If I could only have been there!" he said. "I wish I could be in three places at once."

He meant the bench, the first base coaching line, and the third base line. At this particular time, he was giving the batters orders from the bench. It was one of those incidents which come up in a ball game and have to be decided in the drawing of a breath, so that a manager cannot give orders unless he is right on the spot.

It is my opinion that it is a big advantage to a team to have the manager on the bench rather than in the game.

Frank Chance of the Chicago Cubs is a great leader, but I think he would be a greater one if he could find one of his mechanical ability to play first base, and he could sit on the bench as the director general. He is occupied with the duties of his position and often little things get by him. I believe that we beat the Cubs in two games in 1909 because Chance was playing first base instead of directing the game from the bench.

Frank Chance, Chicago Cubs

In the first contest Ames was pitching and Schlei catching. Now, Schlei was no three hundred hitter, but he was a good man in a pinch and looked like Wagner when compared to Ames as a swatter. Schlei came up to the bat with men on second and third bases, two out, and a chance to win or put us ahead if he could make a hit. The first time it happened, McGraw unfolded his arms and relaxed, which is a sign that he is conceding something for the time being.

"No use," he said. "All those runners are going to waste. We'll have to make another try in the next inning. They will surely pass Schlei to take a chance on Ames."

Then Overall, who was pitching, whistled a strike over the plate and McGraw's body tightened and the old lines around the mouth appeared. Here was a chance yet. "They're going to let him hit," he cried joyfully.

Schlei made a base hit on the next pitch and scored both men. Almost the same thing happened later on in the season with men on second and third bases, and Raymond, another featherweight hitter, pitching. It struck me as being an oversight on the part of Chance on both occasions, probably because he was so busy with his own position and watching the players on the field that he didn't notice the pitcher was the next batter. He let Schlei hit each time, which probably cost him two games.

"Admiral" Schlei, Cincinnati Reds

The Giants were playing St. Louis at the Polo Grounds in 1910, and I was pitching against Harmon. I held the Cardinals to one hit up to the ninth inning, and we had the game won by the score of 1 to 0, when their first batter in the ninth walked. Then, after two had been put out, another scratched a hit. It looked as if we still had the game won, since only one man was left to be put out and the runners were on first and second bases. Mowrey, the red-headed third baseman, came to the bat.

"Murray's playing too near center field for this fellow," remarked McGraw to some of the players on the bench.

Hardly had he said it when Mowrey shoved a long fly to right field, which soared away toward the stand. Murray started to run with the ball. For a minute it looked as if he were going to get there, and then it just tipped his outstretched hands as it fell to the ground. It amounted to a three-base hit and won the game for the Cardinals by the score of 2 to 1.

Mike Mowrey, St. Louis Cardinals

"I knew it," said McGraw, one of who's many roles is as a prophet of evil. "Didn't I call the turn? I ought to have gone out there and stopped the game and moved Murray over. I blame myself for that hit."

That was a game in which the St. Louis batters made three hits and won it. It isn't the number of hits, so much as when they come, that wins ball games. Frequently,

McGraw will stop a game—bring it to a dead standstill—by walking out from the bench as the pitcher is about to wind up.

"Stop it a minute, Meyers," he will shout. "Pull Snodgrass in a little bit for this fellow."

The man interested in statistics would be surprised at how many times little moves of this sort have saved games. But for the McGraw system to be effective, he must have working for him a set of players who are taking the old look around for orders all the time. He has a way of inducing the men to keep their heads up which has worked very well. If a player has been slow or has not taken all the distance McGraw believes is possible on a hit, he often finds $10 less in his pay envelope at the end of the month. And the conversation on the bench at times, when men have made errors of omission, would not fit into any Sunday-school room.

During a game for the most part, McGraw is silent, concentrating his attention on the game, and the players talk in low tones, as if in church, discussing the progress of the contest. But let a player make a bad break, and McGraw delivers a talk to him that would have to be written on asbestos paper.

Arthur Wilson was coaching at third base in one of the games in a series played in Philadelphia the first part of September, 1911. There were barely enough pitchers to go around at the time, and McGraw was very careful to take advantage of every little point, so that nothing would be wasted. He feels that if a game is lost because the other side is better, there is some excuse, but if it goes because some one's head should be used for furniture instead of thinking baseball, it is like losing money that might have been spent. Fletcher was on second base when Meyers came to bat. The Indian pushed the ball to right field along the line. Fletcher came steaming around third base and could have rolled home safely, but Wilson, misjudging the hit, rushed out, tackled him, and threw him back on the bag. Even the plodding Meyers reached second on the hit and McGraw was boiling. He promptly sent a coacher out to relieve Wilson, and his oratory to the young catcher would have made a Billingsgate fishwife sore. We eventually won the game, but at this time there was only a difference of something like one, and it would have been a big relief to have seen that run which Wilson interrupted across the plate.

McGraw is always on Devore's hip because he often feels that this brilliant young player does not get as much out of his natural ability as he might. He is frequently listless, and, often, after a good hit, he will feel satisfied with himself and fan out a couple of times. So, McGraw does all that he can to discourage this self-satisfaction. "Josh" is a great man in a pinch, for he hangs on like a bulldog, and instead of getting nervous, works the harder. If the reader will consult past history, he will note that it was a pinch hit by Devore which won the first world-series game, and one of his wallops, combined with a timely bingle by Crandall, was largely instrumental in bringing the second victory to the Giants. McGraw has made Devore the ball-player that he is by skillful handling. The Giants were having a nip and tuck game with the Cubs in the early part of last summer, when Devore came to the bat in one of those pinches and shot a three bagger over third base which won the game.

As he slid into third and picked himself up, feeling like more or less of a hero because the crowd was announcing this fact to him by prolonged cheers, McGraw said:

"Gee, you're a lucky guy. I wish I had your luck. You were shot full of horseshoes to get that one. When I saw you shut your eyes, I never thought you would hit it."

This was like pricking a bubble, and "Josh's" chest returned to its normal measure. Marquard is another man whom McGraw constantly subjects to a conversational massage. Devore and Marquard room together on the road, and they got to talking about their suite at the hotel during a close game in Philadelphia one day. It annoys McGraw to hear his men discussing off-stage subjects during a critical contest, because it not only distracts their attention, but his and that of the other players.

"Ain't that room of ours a dandy, Rube?" asked Devore.

"Best in the lot," replied Marquard.

"It's got five windows and swell furniture," said Devore.

"Solid mahogany," said McGraw, who apparently had been paying no attention to the conversation. "That is, judging by some of the plays I have seen you two pull. Now can the conversation."

Devore went down into Cuba with the Giants, carrying quite a bank roll from the world's series, and the idea that he was on a picnic. He started a personally conducted tour of Havana on his first night there and we lost the game the next day, "Josh" overlooking several swell opportunities to make hits in pinches. In fact he didn't even get a foul.

"You are fined $25," said McGraw to him after the game.

"You can't fine me," said Devore. "I'm not under contract."

"Then you take the next boat home," replied the manager. "I didn't come down here to let a lot of coffee-colored Cubans show me up. You've got to either play ball or go home."

Devore made four hits the next day.

In giving his signs from the bench to the players, McGraw depends on a gesture or catch word. When "Dummy" Taylor, the deaf and dumb twirler, was with the club, all the players learned the deaf and dumb language. This medium was used for signing for a time, until smart ball players, like Evers and Leach, took up the study of it and became so proficient they could converse fluently on their fingers. But they were also great "listeners," and we didn't discover for some time that this was how they were getting our signs. Thereafter we only used the language for social purposes.

Evers and McGraw got into a conversation one day in the deaf and dumb language at long range and "Johnny" Evers threw a finger out of joint replying to McGraw in a brilliant flash of repartee.

Every successful manager is a distinct type. Each plays the game from the bench. "Connie" Mack gives his men more liberty than most. Chance rules for the most part with an iron hand. Bresnahan is ever spurring his men on. Chance changes his seat on the bench, and there is a double steal. "Connie" Mack uncrosses his legs, and the hit and run is tried.

"Johnny" Evers, Chicago Cubs

Most managers transmit their signs by movements or words. Jennings is supposed to have hidden in his jumble of jibes some catch words.

The manager on the bench must know just when to change pitchers. He has to decide the exact time to send in a substitute hitter, when to install another base runner. All these decisions must be made in the "batting" of an eye. It takes quick and accurate judgment, and the successful manager must be right usually. That's playing the game from the bench.

# Coaching Good and Bad

*Coaching is Divided into Three Parts: Offensive, Defensive, and the Use of Crowds to Rattle Players—Why McGraw Developed Scientific Coaching—The Important Role a Coacher Plays in the Crisis of a Big-League Ball Game when, on his Orders, Hangs Victory or Defeat.*

**CRITICAL** MOMENTS occur in every close ball game, when coaching may win or lose it.

"That wasn't the stage for you to try to score," yelled John McGraw, the manager of the Giants, at "Josh" Devore, as the New York left-fielder attempted to count from second base on a short hit to left field, with no one out and the team one run behind in a game with the Pirates one day in 1911, when every contest might mean the winning or losing of the pennant.

"First time in my life I was ever thrown out trying to score from second on a base hit to the outfield," answered Devore, "and besides the coacher sent me in."

"I don't care," replied McGraw, "that was a two out play."

As a matter of fact, one of the younger players on the team was coaching at third base at the time and made an error of judgment in sending Devore home, of which an older head would not have been guilty. And the Pirates beat us by just that one run the coacher sacrificed. The next batter came through with an outfield fly which would have scored Devore from third base easily.

Probably no more wily general ever crouched on the coaching line at third base than John McGraw. His judgment in holding runners or urging them on to score is almost uncanny. Governed by no set rules himself, he has formulated a list of regulations for his players which might be called the "McGraw Coaching Curriculum." He has favorite expressions, such as "there are stages" and "that was a two out play," which mean certain chances are to be taken by a coacher at one point in a contest, while to attempt such a play under other circumstances would be nothing short of foolhardy.

With the development of baseball, coaching has advanced until it is now an exact science. For many years the two men who stood at first and third bases were stationed there merely to bullyrag and abuse the pitchers, often using language that was a disgrace to a ball field. When they were not busy with this part of their art, they handed helpful hints to the runners as to where the ball was and whether the second baseman was concealing it under his shirt (a favorite trick of the old days), while the pitcher pretended to prepare to deliver it. But as rules were made which strictly forbade the use of indecent language to a pitcher, and as the old school of clowns passed, coaching developed into a science, and the sentries stationed at first and third bases found themselves occupying important jobs.

For some time, McGraw frowned down upon scientific coaching, until its value was forcibly brought home to him one day by an incident that occurred at the Polo Grounds, and since then he has developed it until his knowledge of advising base runners is the pinnacle of scientific coaching.

A few years ago, the Giants were having a nip and tuck struggle one day, when Harry McCormick, then the left-fielder, came to the plate and knocked the ball to the old center-field ropes. He sped around the bases, and when he reached third, it looked as if he could roll home ahead of the ball. "Cy" Seymour was coaching and surprised everybody by rushing out and tackling McCormick, throwing him down and trying to force him back to third base. But big McCormick got the best of the struggle, scrambled to his feet, and finally scored after overcoming the obstacle that Seymour made. That run won the game.

"What was the matter with you, Cy?" asked McGraw as Seymour came to the bench after he had almost lost the game by his poor coaching.

"The sun got in my eyes, and I couldn't see the ball," replied Seymour.

"You'd better wear smoked glasses the next time you go out to coach," replied the manager.

The batter was hitting the ball due east, and the game was being played in the afternoon, so Seymour had no alibi. From the moment "Cy" made that mistake, McGraw realized the value of scientific coaching, which means making the most of every hit in a game.

I have always held that a good actor with a knowledge of baseball would make a good coacher, because it is the acting that impresses a base runner, not the talking.

More often than not, the conversation of a coacher, be it ever so brilliant, is not audible above the screeching of the crowd at critical moments. And I believe that McGraw is a great actor, at least of the baseball school. The cheering of the immense crowds which attend ball games, if it can be organized, is a potent factor in winning or losing them. McGraw gets the most out of a throng by his clever acting. Did any patron of the Polo Grounds ever see him turn to the stands or make any pretense that he was paying attention to the spectators? Does he ever play to the gallery? Yet it is admitted that he can do more with a crowd, make it more malleable, than any other man in baseball to-day.

The attitude of the spectators makes a lot of difference to a ball club. A lackadaisical, half-interested crowd often results in the team playing slovenly ball, while a lively throng can inject ginger into the men and put the whole club on its toes. McGraw is skilled in getting the most out of the spectators without letting them know that he is doing it.

Did you ever watch the little manager crouching, immovable, at third base with a mitt on his hand, when the New York club goes to bat in the seventh inning two runs behind? The first hitter gets a base on balls.

McGraw leaps into the air, kicks his heels together, claps his mitt, shouts at the umpire, runs in and pats the next batter on the back, and says something to the pitcher. The crowd gets it cue, wakes up and leaps into the air, kicking its heels together. The whole atmosphere inside the park is changed in a minute, and the air is bristling with enthusiasm. The other coacher, at first base, is waving his hands and running up and down the line, while the men on the bench have apparently gained new hope. They are moving about restlessly, and the next two hitters are swinging their bats in anticipation with a vigor which augurs ill for the pitcher. The game has found Ponce de Leon's fountain of youth, and the little, silent actor on the third base coaching line is the cause of the change.

"Nick" Altrock, the old pitcher on the Chicago White Sox, was one of the most skillful men at handling a crowd that the game has ever developed. As a pitcher, Altrock was largely instrumental in bringing a world's championship to the American League team in 1906, and, as a coacher, after his Big-League pitching

"Nick" Altrock, Chicago White Sox

days were nearly done, he won many a game by his work on the lines in pinches. Baseball has produced several comedians, some with questionable ratings as humorists.

"Germany" Schaefer, Washington Senators

There is "Germany" Schaefer of the Washington team, and there were "Rube" Waddell, "Bugs" Raymond and others, but "Nick" Altrock could give the best that the game has brought out in the way of comic-supplement players a terrible battle for the honors.

At the old south side park in Chicago, I have seen him go to the lines with a catcher's mitt and a first-baseman's glove on his hands and lead the untrained mob as skillfully as one of those pompadoured young men with a megaphone does the undergraduates at a college football game.

My experience as a pitcher has been that it is not the steady, unbroken flood of howling and yelling, with the incessant pounding of feet, that gets on the nerves of a ball-player, but the broken, rhythmical waves of sound or the constant reiteration of one expression. A man gets accustomed to the steady cheering. It becomes a part of the game and his surroundings, as much as the stands and the crowd itself are, and he does not know that it is there. Let the coacher be clever enough to induce a crowd to repeat over and over just one sentence such as

"Get a hit," "Get a hit," and it wears on the steadiest nerves. Nick Altrock had his baseball chorus trained so that, by a certain motion of the arm, he could get the crowd to do this at the right moment.

But the science of latter-day coaching means much more than using the crowd. All coaching, like all Gaul and four or five other things, is divided into three parts, defensive coaching, offensive coaching, and the use of the crowd. Offensive coaching means the handling of base runners and requires quick and accurate judgment. The defensive sort is the advice that one player on the field gives another as to where to throw the ball, who shall take a hit, and how the base runner is coming into the bag.

There is a sub-division of defensive coaching which might be called the illegitimate brand. It is giving "phoney" advice to a base runner by the fielders of the other side that may lead him, in the excitement of the moment, to make a foolish play. This style has developed largely in the Big-Leagues in the last three or four years.

Offensive coaching, in my opinion, is the most important. For a man to be a good coacher he must be trained for the work. The best coaches are the seasoned players, the veterans of the game. A man must know the throwing ability of each outfielder on the opposing club, he must be familiar with the speed of the base runner whom he is handling, and he must be so closely acquainted with the game as a whole that he knows the stages at which to try a certain play and the circumstances under which the same attempt would be foolish. Above all things, he must be a quick thinker.

Watch McGraw on the coaching lines someday. As he crouches, he picks up a pebble and throws it out of his way, and two base runners start a double steal. "Hughie" Jennings emits his famous "Ee- Yaah!" and the third baseman creeps in, expecting Cobb to bunt with a man on first base and no one out. The hitter pushes the ball on a line past the third baseman. The next time Jennings shrieks his famous war-cry, it has a different intonation, and the batter bunts.

"Bill" Dahlen of the Brooklyn club shouts, "Watch his foot," and the base runner starts while the batter smashes the ball on a hit and run play. Again, the pitcher hears that "Watch his foot." He "wastes one," so that the batter will not get a chance at the ball and turns to first base. He is surprised to find the runner anchored there.

"Bill" Dahlen, Brooklyn Superbas

Nothing has happened. So, it will be seen that the offensive coacher controls the situation and directs the plays, usually taking his orders from the manager, if the boss himself is not on the lines.

In 1911 the Giants led the National League by a good margin in stealing bases, and to this speed many critics attributed the fact that the championship was won by the club. I can safely say that every base which was pilfered by a New York runner was stolen by the direct order of McGraw, except in the few games from which he was absent. Then his lieutenants followed his system as closely as anyone can pursue the involved and intricate style that he alone understands. If it was the base running of the Giants that won the pennant for the club, then it was the coaching of McGraw, employing the speed of his men and his opportunities, which brought the championship to New York.

The first thing that every manager teaches his players now is to obey absolutely the orders of the coacher, and then he selects able men to give the advice. The brain of McGraw is behind each game the Giants play, and he plans every move, most of the hitters going to the plate with definite instructions from him as to what to try to do. In order to make this system efficient, absolute discipline must be assured.

If a player has other ideas than McGraw as to what should be done, "Mac's" invariable answer to him is: "You do what I tell you, and I'll take the responsibility if we lose."

For two months at the end of 1911, McGraw would not let either "Josh" Devore or John Murray swing at a first ball pitched to them. Murray did this one day, after he had been ordered not to, and he was promptly fined $10 and sat down on the bench, while Becker played right field. Many fans doubtless recall the substitution of Becker but could not understand the move.

Murray and Devore are what are known in baseball as "first-ball hitters." That is, they invariably hit at the first one delivered. They watch a pitcher wind up and swing their bats involuntarily, as a man blinks his eyes when he sees a blow started. It is probably due to slight nervousness. The result was that the news of this weakness spread rapidly around the circuit by the underground routes of baseball, and every pitcher in the League was handing Devore and Murray a bad ball on the first one. Of course, each would miss it or else make a dinky little hit. They were always "in the hole," which means that the pitcher had the advantage in the count. McGraw became exasperated after Devore had fanned out three times one day by getting bad starts, hitting at the first ball.

"After this," said McGraw to both Murray and Devore in the clubhouse, "if either of you moves his bat off his shoulder at a first ball, even if it cuts the plate, you will be fined $10 and sat down."

Murray forgot the next day, saw the pitcher wind up, and swung his bat at the first one. He spent the rest of the month on the bench. But Devore's hitting improved at once because all the pitchers, expecting him to swing at the first one, were surprised to find him "taking it" and, as it was usually bad, he had the pitcher constantly "in the hole," instead of being at a disadvantage himself. For this reason, he was able to guess more accurately what the pitcher was going to throw, and his hitting consequently improved. So did Murray's after he had served his term on the bench. The right-fielder hit well up to the world's series and then he just struck a slump that any player is liable to encounter. But so dependent is McGraw's system on absolute discipline for its success that he dispensed with the services of a good player for a month to preserve his style.

In contrast, "Connie" Mack, the manager of the Athletics, and by many declared to be the greatest leader in the country (although each private, of course, is true to his own general), lets his players use their own judgment largely. He seldom gives a batter a direct order unless the pinch is very stringent.

The most difficult position to fill as a coacher is at third base, the critical corner. There a man's judgment must be lightning fast and always accurate. He encourages runners with his voice, but his orders are given primarily with his hands, because often the noise made by the crowd drowns out the shouted instructions. Last, he must be prepared to handle all sorts of base running. On nearly every ball club, there are some players who are known in the frank parlance of the profession as "hog wild runners."

The expression means that these players are bitten by a sort of "bug" which causes them to lose their heads when once they get on the bases. They cannot be stopped, oftentimes fighting with a coacher to go on to the next base, when it is easy to see that if the attempt is made, the runner is doomed.

New York fans have often seen McGraw dash out into the line at third base, tackle Murray, and throw him back on the bag. He is a "hog wild" runner, and with him on the bases, the duties of a coacher become more arduous. He will insist on scoring if he is not stopped or does not drop dead.

Some youngster was coaching on third base in a game with Boston in the summer of 1911 and the Giants had a comfortable lead of several runs. Murray was on second when the batter hit clearly and sharply to left field.

Murray started, and, with his usual intensity of purpose, rounded third base at top speed, bound to score. The ball was already on the way home when Murray, about ten feet from the bag, tripped and fell. He scrambled safely back to the cushion on all fours. There was nothing else to do.

"This is his third year with me," laughed McGraw on the bench, "and that's the first time he has ever failed to try to score from second base on a hit unless he was tackled."

All ball clubs have certain "must" motions which are as strictly observed as danger signals on a railroad. A coacher's hand upraised will stop a base runner as abruptly as the uplifted white glove of a traffic policeman halts a row of automobiles. A wave of the arm will start a runner going at top speed again.

Many times, a quick-witted ball-player wins a game for his club by his snap judgment. Again, McGraw is the master of that. He took a game from the Cubs in 1911, because always alert for flaws in the opposition, he noticed the center-fielder drop his arm after getting set to throw the ball home. Devore was on second base, and one run was needed to win the game. Doyle hit sharply to center field, and Devore, coming from second, started to slow up as he rounded third. Hofman, the Chicago center-fielder, perceiving this slackening of pace, dropped his arm. McGraw noticed this, and, with a wave of his arm, notified Devore to go home. With two strides he was at top speed again, and Hofman, taken by surprise, threw badly.

The run scored which won the game.

The pastime of bullyragging the pitcher by the coaches has lost its popularity recently. The wily coacher must first judge the temperament of a pitcher before he dares to undertake to get on his nerves. Clark Griffith, formerly the manager of Cincinnati, has a reputation for being able to ruin young pitchers just attempting to establish themselves in the Big-League. Time and again he has forced youngsters back to the minors by his constant cry of "Watch his foot" or "He's going to waste this one."

Photo by L. Van Oeyen, Cleveland, Ohio
*Baker out at the plate trying to stretch a triple into a home run.*

This picture shows Catcher Easterly of Cleveland waiting with the ball to touch Baker. The home-run hero of the Athletics is shown in the picture starting the fall-away slide in an effort to get away from Easterly. Harry Davis is approaching the plate, and Jack Sheridan is awaiting the outcome at the plate.

The rules are very strict now about talking to pitchers, but, if a complaint is made, Griffith declares that he was warning the batter that it was to be a pitchout, which is perfectly legitimate. The rules permit the coacher to talk to the batter and the base runners.

Griffith caught a Tartar in Grover Cleveland Alexander, the sensational pitcher of the Philadelphia club. It was at his first appearance in Cincinnati that the young fellow got into the hole with several men on the bases, and "Mike" Mitchell coming up to the bat.

"Now here is where we get a look at the 'yellow,'" yelled Griffith at Alexander. The young pitcher walked over toward third base.

"I'm going to make that big boob up at the bat there show such a 'yellow streak' that you won't be able to see any white," declared Alexander, and then he struck Mitchell out.

Griffith had tried the wrong tactics.

A story is told of Fred Clarke and "Rube" Waddell, the eccentric twirler. Waddell was once one of the best pitchers in the business when he could concentrate his attention on his work, but his mind wandered easily.

"Now pay no attention to Clarke," warned his manager before the game.

Clarke tried everything from cajolery to abuse on Waddell with no effect, because the eccentric "Rube" had been tipped to fight shy of the Pittsburg manager. Suddenly Clarke became friendly and walked with Waddell between innings, chatting on trivial matters.

At last, he said: "Why don't you come out on my ranch in Kansas and hunt after the season, George? I've got a dog out there you might train." "What kind of a dog?" asked Waddell at once interested.

"Just a pup," replied Clarke, "and you can have him if he takes a fancy to you."

"They all do," replied Waddell. "He's as good as mine."

The next inning the big left-hander was still thinking of that dog, and the Pirates made five runs.

In many instances defensive coaching is as important as the offensive brand, which simply indorses the old axiom that any chain is only as strong as its weakest link or any ball club is only as efficient as its most deficient department.

When Roger Bresnahan was on the Giants, he was one of those aggressive players who are always coaching the other fielders and holding a team together, a type so much desired by a manager. If a slow roller was hit between the pitcher's box and third base, I could always hear "Rog" yelling, "You take it,

Roger Bresnahan, New York Giants

Matty," or, "Artie, Artie," meaning Devlin, the third baseman. He was in a position to see which man would be better able to make the play, and he gave this helpful advice. His coaching saved many a game for the Giants in the old days.

"Al" Bridwell, the former shortstop, was of the same type, and, if you have ever attended a ball game at the Polo Grounds, you have doubtless heard him in his shrill, piercing voice, shouting: "I've got it! I've got it!" or, "You take it!"

This style of coaching saves ballplayers from accidents, and accidents have lost many a pennant. I have always held that it was a lack of the proper coaching that sent "Cy" Seymour, formerly the Giant center-fielder, out of the Big-Leagues and back to the minors. Both Murray and he attempted to catch the same fly in the season of 1909 and came into collision. Seymour went down on the field, but later got up and played the game out. However, he hurt his leg so badly that it never regained its strength.

Then there is that other style of defensive coaching which is the shouting of misleading advice by the fielders to the base runners. Collins and Barry, the second baseman and shortstop on the Athletics, worked a clever trick in one of the games of the 1911 world's series which illustrates my point. The play is as old as the one in which the second baseman hides the ball under his shirt so as to catch a man asleep off first base, but often the old ones are the more effective.

Doyle was on first base in one of the contests played in Philadelphia, and the batter lifted a short foul fly to Baker, playing third base. The crowd roared and the coacher's voice was drowned by the volume of sound. "Eddie" Collins ran to cover second base, and Barry scrabbled his hand along the dirt as if preparing to field a ground ball.

Larry Doyle, New York Giants

"Throw it here! Throw it here!" yelled Collins, and Doyle, thinking that they were trying for a force play, increased his efforts to reach second. Baker caught the fly, and Larry was doubled up at first base so far that he looked foolish. Yet it really was not his fault. The safest thing for a base runner to do under those circumstances is to get one glimpse of the coacher's motions and then he can tell whether to go back or to go on.

"Johnnie" Kling, the old catcher of the Chicago Cubs, used to work a clever piece of defensive coaching with John Evers, the second baseman. This was tried on young players and usually was successful. The victim was picked out before the game, and the play depended upon him arriving at second base.

"Johnnie" Kling, Chicago Cubs

Once there the schemers worked it as follows:
When the "busher" was found taking a large lead, Evers would dash to the bag and Kling would make a bluff to throw the ball but hold it. The runner naturally scampered for the base. Then, seeing that Kling had not thrown, he would start to walk away from it again.

"If the Jew had thrown that time, he would have had you," Evers would carelessly hurl over his shoulder at the intended victim.

The man usually turned for a fatal second to reply. Tinker, who was playing shortstop, rushed in from behind, Kling whipped the ball to the bag, and the man, caught off his guard, was tagged out. The play was really made before the game when the victim was selected.

It was this same Evers-Kling combination that turned the tide in the first inning of the most famous game ever played in baseball, the extra one between the Giants and the Cubs in the season of 1908.

The Chicago club was nervous in the first inning. Tenney was hit by a pitched ball, and Herzog walked. It looked as if Pfeister, the Chicago pitcher, was losing his grip. Bresnahan struck out, and Kling, always alert, dropped the third strike, but conveniently at his feet. Thinking that here was an opportunity the crowd roared. Evers, playing deep, almost behind Herzog, shouted, "Go on!"

Herzog took the bait in the excitement of the moment and ran—and was nipped many yards from first base. There are many tricks to the coacher's trade, both offensive and defensive, and it is the quickest-witted man who is the best coacher. The sentry at first yells as the pitcher winds up, "There he goes!" imitating the first baseman as nearly as possible, in the hope that the twirler will waste one by pitching out and thus give the batter an advantage.

Buck Herzog, New York Giants

The coacher on third base will shout at the runner on a short hit to the outfield, "Take your turn!" in the dim hope that the fielder, seeing the man rounding third, will throw the ball home, and the hitter can thus make an extra base. And the job of coaching is no sinecure. McGraw has told me after directing a hard game that he is as tired as if he had played.

# Honest and Dishonest Sign Stealing

*Everything Fair in Baseball except the Dishonest Stealing of Signals—The National Game More a Contest of the Wits than Most Onlookers Imagine.*

**WHEN THE** Philadelphia Athletics unexpectedly defeated the Chicago Cubs in the world's series of 1910, the National League players cried that their signals had been stolen by the American League team, and that, because Connie Mack's batters knew what to expect, they had won the championship.

But were the owners or any member of the Philadelphia club arrested charged with grand larceny in stealing the baseball championship of the world? No. Was there any murmur against the methods of Connie Mack's men? No, again. By a strange kink in the ethics of baseball John Kling, the Chicago catcher, was blamed by the other players on the defeated team for the signs being stolen. They charged that he had been careless in covering his signals and that the enemy's coachers, particularly Topsy Hartsell, a clever man at it, had seen them from the lines. This was really the cause of Kling leaving the Cubs and going to Boston in 1911.

After the games were over and the series was lost, many of the players, and especially the pitchers, would hardly speak to Kling, the man who had as much as anyone else to do with the Cubs winning four championships, and the man who by his great throwing had made the reputations of a lot of their pitchers. But the players were sore because they had lost the series and lost the extra money which many of them had counted as their own before the games started, and they looked around for someone to blame and found Kling.

One of the pitchers complained after he had lost a game: "Can't expect a guy to win with his catcher giving the signs so the coaches can read 'em and tip the batters." "And you can't expect a catcher to win a game for you if you haven't got anything on the ball," replied Kling, for he is quick tempered and cannot stand reflections on his ability.

But the pitcher's chance remark had given the other players an excuse for fixing the blame, and it was put on Kling.

I honestly do not believe that Kling was in any way responsible for the rout of the proud Cubs. The Chicago pitchers were away off form in the series and could not control the ball, thus getting themselves "into the hole" all the time. Shrewd Connie Mack soon realized this and ordered his batters to wait everything out, to make the twirlers throw every ball possible. The result was that, with the pitcher continually in the hole, the batters were guessing what was coming and frequently guessing right, as any smart hitter could under the circumstances. This made it look as if the Athletics were getting the Cubs' signals.

"Why, I changed signs every three innings, Matty," Kling told me afterwards in discussing the charge. "Some of the boys said that I gave the old bended-knee sign for a curve ball. Well, did you ever find anything to improve on the old ones? That's why they are old."

But the Cubs still point the finger of scorn at Kling, for it hurts to lose. I know it, I have lost myself. Even though the Athletics are charged with stealing the signs whether they did or not, it is no smirch on the character of the club, for they stole honestly—which sounds like a paradox.

"You have such jolly funny morals in this bally country," declared an Englishman I once met. "You steal and rob in baseball and yet you call it fair. Now in cricket we give our opponents every advantage, don't cher know, and after the game we are all jolly good fellows at tea together."

This brings us down to the ethics of signal stealing. Each game has its own recognized standards of fairness. For instance, no tricks are tolerated in tennis, yet the baseball manager who can devise some scheme by which he disconcerts his opponents is considered a great leader. I was about to say that all is fair in love, war, and baseball, but will modify that too comprehensive statement by saying all is fair in love, war, and baseball except stealing signals dishonestly, which listens like another paradox. Therefore, I shall divide the subject of signal stealing into half portions, the honest and the dishonest halves, and, since we are dealing in paradoxes, take up the latter first.

Dishonest signal stealing might be defined as obtaining information by artificial aids. The honest methods are those requiring cleverness of eye, mind, and hand without outside assistance. One of the most flagrant and for a time successful pieces of signal stealing occurred in Philadelphia several years ago.

Opposing players can usually tell when the batsman is getting the signs, because he steps up and sets himself for a curve with so much confidence. During the season of 1899 the report went around the circuit that the Philadelphia club was stealing signals, because the batters were popping them all on the nose, but no one was able to discover the transmitter. The coaches were closely watched and it was evident that these sentinels were not getting the signs.

It was while the Washington club, then in the National League, was playing Philadelphia that there came a rainy morning which made the field very wet, and for a long time it was doubtful whether a game could be played in the afternoon, but the Washington club insisted on it and overruled the protests of the Phillies. Arlie Latham, now the coacher on the Giants', was playing third base for the Senators at the time. He has told me often since how he discovered the device by which the signs were being stolen. He repeated the story to me recently when I asked him for the facts to use in this book.

"There was a big puddle in the third base coaching box that day," said Latham. "And it was in the third inning that I noticed Cupid Childs, the Philadelphia second baseman, coaching. He stood with one foot in the puddle and never budged it, although the water came up to his shoe-laces. He usually jumped around when on the lines, and this stillness surprised me.

Arlie Latham, Washington Senators

"Better go get your rubbers if you are goin' to keep that trilby there," I said to him. "Charley horse and the rheumatism have no terrors for you."

But he kept his foot planted in the puddle just the same, and first thing the batter cracked out a base hit.

"So that's where you're gettin' the signs?" I said to him, not guessing that it really was.

Then he started to jump around and we got the next two batters out right quick, there being a big slump in the Philadelphia hitting as soon as he took his foot out of that puddle.

"When the Washington club went to bat, I hiked out to the third base line and started to coach, putting my foot into the puddle as near the place where Childs had had his as I could. "'Here's where we get a few signs,' I yelled, "And I ain't afraid of Charley horse, either."

I looked over at the Philadelphia bench, and there were all the extra players sitting with their caps pulled down over their eyes, so that I couldn't see their faces. The fielders all looked the other way. Then I knew I was on a warm scent.

When the Washington players started back for the field I told Tommy Corcoran that I thought they must be getting the signs from the third base coaching box, although I hadn't been able to feel anything there. He went over and started pawing around in the dirt and water with his spikes and fingers. Pretty soon he dug up a square chunk of wood with a buzzer on the underside of it.

Tommy Corcoran, New York Giants

"That ought to help their hitting a little," he remarked as he kept on pulling.

Up came a wire, and when he started to pull on it he found that it was buried about an inch under the soil and ran across the outfield. He kept right on coiling it up and following it, like a hound on a scent, the Philadelphia players being very busy all this time and nervous like a busher at his debut into Big-League society. One of the substitutes started to run for the clubhouse, but I stopped him.

Tommy was galloping by this time across the outfield and all the time pulling up this wire. It led straight to the clubhouse, and there sitting where he could get a good view of the catcher's signs with a pair of field-glasses was Morgan Murphy. The wire led right to him.

Morgan Murphy, Philadelphia Athletics

"What cher doin'?" asked Tommy. "Watchin' the game," replied Murphy.

"Couldn't you see it easier from the bench than lookin' through those peepers from here? And why are you connected up with this machine?" inquired Tommy, showin' him the chunk of wood with the buzzer attached.

"I guess you've got the goods," Murphy answered with a laugh, and all the newspapers laughed at it then, too.

But the batting averages of the Philadelphia players took an awful slump after that.

"Why didn't they tip me?" asked Murphy as he put aside his field-glasses and went to the bench and watched the rest of the game from there. And we later won that contest, our first victory of the series, which was no discredit to us, since it was "like gamblin' against loaded dice," concluded Arlie.

The newspapers may have laughed at the incident in those days, but since that time the National Commission has intimated that if there was ever a recurrence of such tactics, the club caught using them would be subjected to a heavy fine and possibly expulsion from the League. So much have baseball standards improved.

The incident is a great illustration of the unfair method of obtaining signs. Since then, there have come from time-to-time reports of teams taking signals by mechanical devices. The Athletics once declared that the American League team in New York had a man stationed behind the fence in center field with a pair of glasses and that he shifted a line in the score board slightly, so as to tip off the batters, but this charge was never confirmed. It was said a short time ago that the Athletics themselves had a spy located in a house outside their grounds and that he tipped the batters by raising and lowering an awning a trifle. When the Giants went to Philadelphia in 1911 for the first game of the world's series in the enemy's camp, I kept watching the windows of the houses just outside of the park for suspicious movements but could discover none.

Once in Pittsburg I thought that the Pirates were getting the Giants' signals and I kept my eyes glued to the score board in center field, throughout one whole series, to see if any of the figures moved or changed positions, as that seemed to be the only place from which a batter could be tipped. But I never discovered anything wrong.

There are many fair ways to steal the signs of the enemy, so many that the smart ball-player is always kept on the alert by them. Baseball geniuses, some almost magicians, are constantly looking for new schemes to find out what the catcher is telling the pitcher, what the batter is tipping the base runner to, or what the coacher's instructions are. The Athletics have a great reputation as being a club able to get the other team's signs if they are obtainable. This is their record all around the American League circuit.

Personally, I do not believe that Connie Mack's players steal as much information as they get the credit for, but the reputation itself, if they never get a sign, is valuable. If a prizefighter is supposed to have a haymaking punch in his left hand, the other fellow is going to be constantly looking out for that left. If the players on a club have great reputations as signal stealers, their opponents are going to be on their guard all the time, which gives the team with the reputation just that much advantage. If a pitcher has a reputation, he has the percentage on the batter. Therefore, this gossip about the signal-stealing ability of the Athletics has added to their natural strength.

"Bill," I said to Dahlen, the Brooklyn manager, one day toward the end of the season of 1911, when the Giants were playing their schedule out after the pennant was sure, "see if you can get the Chief's signs."

Dahlen coached on first base and then went to third, always looking for Meyers's signals.

Pretty soon he came to me. "I can see them a little bit, Matty," he reported.

"Chief," I said to Meyers that night as I buttonholed him in the clubhouse, "you've got to be careful to cover up your signs in the Big Series. The Athletics have a reputation of being pretty slick at getting them. And to make sure we will arrange a set of signs that I can give if we think they are 'hep' to yours."

So right there Meyers and I fixed up a code of signals that I could give to him, the Chief always to use some himself which would be "phoney" of course and might have the desirable effect of "crossing them."

In the first championship game at the Polo Grounds, Topsy Hartsell was out on the coaching lines looking for signals, and the Chief started giving the real ones until Davis stepped into a curve ball and cracked it to left field for a single, scoring the only run made by the Athletics.

*Topsy Hartsel, Philadelphia Athletics*

Right here Meyers stopped, and I began transmitting the private information, although the Chief continued to pass out signals that meant nothing. The Athletics were getting the Indian's and could not understand why the answers seemed invariably to be wrong, for a couple of them struck out swinging at bad balls, and one batter narrowly avoided being hit by a fast one when apparently, he had been tipped off to a curve and was set ready to swing at it.

They did not discover that I was behind the signals, although to make this method successful the catcher must be a clever man. If he makes it too obvious that his signals are "phoney" and are meant to be seen, then the other club will look around for the source of the real ones. Meyers carefully concealed his misleading wig-wags beneath his chest protector, under his glove and behind his knee, as any good catcher does his real signs, so they would not look at my head.

Many persons argue: if a man sees the signs, what good does it do him if he does not know what they mean? It is easy for a smart ballplayer to deduce the answers because there are only three real signs passed between a pitcher and catcher, the sign for the fast one, for the curve ball and for the pitchout. If a coacher sees a catcher open his hand behind his glove and then watches the pitcher throw a fast one, he is likely to guess that the open palm says, "Fast one."

After a coacher has stolen the desired information, he must be clever to pass it along to the batter without the other club being aware that he is doing it. He may straighten up to tell the batter a curve ball is coming, and bend over to forecast a fast one, and turn his back as a neutral signal, meaning that he does not know what is coming. If a coacher is smart enough to pass the meanings to the batter without the other team getting on, he may go through the entire season as a transmitter of information. To steal signs fairly requires quickness of mind, eye and action. Few players can do it successfully. Perhaps that is why it is considered fair.

If a team is going to make a success of signal stealing it must get every sign that is given, for an occasional crumb of information picked up at random is worse than none at all.

First, it is dangerous. A batter, tipped off that a curved ball is coming, steps up to the plate and is surprised to meet a fast one, which often he has not time to dodge. Many a good ball-player has been injured in this way, and an accident to a star has cost more than one pennant.

"Joe" Kelley, formerly manager of the Reds, was coaching in Cincinnati one day several years ago, and "Eagle Eye Jake" Beckley, the old first baseman and a chronic three hundred hitter, was at the bat. I had been feeding him low drops and Kelley, on the third base line, thought he was getting the signals that Jack Warner, the Giant catcher in a former cast of characters, was giving. I saw Kelley apparently pass some information to Beckley, and the latter stepped almost across the plate ready for a curve. He encountered a high, fast one, close in, and he encountered it with that part of him between his neck and hat band. "Eagle Eye" was unconscious for two days after that and in the hospital several weeks.

"Eagle Eye" Jake Beckley, Cincinnati Reds

When he got back into the game he said to me one day: "Why didn't you throw me that curve, Matty, that 'Joe' tipped me to?"

"Were you tipped off?" I asked. "Then it was 'Joe's' error, not mine."

"Say," he answered, "if I ever take another sign from a coacher I hope the ball kills me."

"It probably will," I replied. "That one nearly did."

It is one of the risks of signal stealing. Beckley had received the wrong information and I felt no qualms at hitting him, for it was not a wild pitch but a misinterpreted signal which had put him out of the game. His manager, not I, was to blame.

For this reason, many nervous players refuse to accept any information from a coacher, even if the coacher thinks he knows what is going to be pitched, because they do not dare take the risk of getting hit by a fast one, against which they have little protection if set for a curve.

On this account few National League clubs attempt to steal signs as a part of the regular teamwork, but many individuals make a practice of it for their own benefit and for the benefit of the batter, if he is not of the timid type.

As soon as a runner gets on second base he is in an excellent position to see the hands of the catcher, and it is then that the man behind the bat is doing all that he can cover up. Jack Warner, the old Giant, used sometimes to give his

Jack Warner, New York Giants

signals with his mouth in this emergency, because they were visible from the pitcher's box, but not from second base. The thieves were looking at his hands for them.

In the National League, Leach, Clarke, Wagner, Bresnahan, Evers, Tinker and a few more of the sort are dangerous to have on second. Wagner will get on the middle sack and watch the catcher until he thinks that he has discovered the pitchout sign, which means a ball is to be wasted in the hope that a base runner can be caught. Wagner takes a big lead, and the catcher, tempted, gives the "office" to waste one, thinking to nail "Hans" off second. The Dutchman sees it, and instead of running back to second dashes for third. He starts as the catcher lets go of the ball to throw to second and can usually make the extra base.

Many coaches, who do not attempt to get the signs for fast and curved balls, study the catcher to get his pitchout sign, because once this is recognized it gives the team at the bat a great advantage. If a coacher sees the catcher give the pitchout signal, he can stop the runner from trying to steal and the pitcher has wasted a ball and is "in the hole." Then if his control is uncertain the result is likely to be disastrous.

Several players in the National League are always trying to get the batter's signs. Bresnahan, the manager and catcher of the St. Louis club, devotes half his time and energy to looking for the wireless code employed by batter and base runner. If he can discover the hit and run sign, then he is able to order a pitchout and catch the man who has started to run in response to it several feet at second base. He is a genius at getting this information. Once late in 1911, when the New York club was in St. Louis on the last trip West, I came up to the bat with Fletcher on first base.

I rubbed the end of my stick with my hand and Roger exclaimed: "Why, that's your old hit and run, Matty! What are you trying to do, kid me?"

"I forgot you knew it, Rog," I answered, "but it goes."

He thought I was attempting to cross him and did not order a pitchout. The sign had been given intentionally. I hit the ball and had the laugh on him. If a catcher can get a pitchout on a hit and run sign he upsets the other team greatly. Take a fast man on first base and the batter signs him that he is going to hit the next ball. The runner gets his start and the ball comes up so wide that the batter could not half reach it with a ten-foot bat. The runner is caught easily at second base and it makes him look foolish. That is why so many catchers devote time to looking for this signal. It is a great fruit bearer.
Many of the extra players on the bench are always on the alert for the hit and run sign.

This is a typical situation:
The Giants were playing the Pittsburg club one day in 1911. Byrne was on first base. Fred Clarke was at bat and Byrne started for second while Clarke hit the ball to right field, Byrne reaching third base on the play.

"What did he do?" asked Ames.

"Did you get it, Matty?" inquired Wiltse.

"No," I answered. "Did you?"

"I think he tapped his bat on the plate," replied Wiltse.

The next time Clarke came up we were all looking to see if he tapped his bat on the plate. Byrne was again on first base. The Pirates' manager fixed his cap, he stepped back out of the box and knocked the dirt out of his cleats, and he did two or three other natural things before the pitch, but nothing happened. Then he tapped his bat on the plate.

"Make him put them over, Chief," yelled Wiltse which, translated, meant, "Order a pitch-out, Chief. He just gave Byrne the hit and run sign."

Meyers signed for a pitchout, and Byrne was caught ten feet from second. Wiltse on the bench had really nailed the base runner. As soon as a sign is discovered it is communicated to the other players, and they

Hooks Wiltse, New York Giants

are always watching for it, but try to conceal the fact that they recognize it, because, as soon as a batter discovers that his messages are being read, he changes his code.

From these few facts about signals and sign stealing some idea of the battle of wits that is going on between two ball clubs in a game may be obtained. That is why so few men without brains last in the Big-Leagues nowadays. A young fellow broke in with the Giants a few years ago and was very anxious to make good. He was playing shortstop.

"Watch for the catcher's signs and then shift," McGraw told him one day.

It is well known in baseball that a right-handed hitter will naturally push a curve over the outside corner of the plate toward right field and over the inside he will pull it around toward third base. But this youngster was overanxious and would shift before the pitcher started to deliver the ball. Some smart player on another club noticed this and tipped the batters off to watch the youngster for the signs. When he shifted toward second base the batter set himself for a ball over the outside corner. For a long time, McGraw could not understand how the other teams were getting the Giants' signs, especially as it was on our home grounds. At last, he saw the new infielder shift one day and the batter prepare for an inside ball.

"Say," he said to the player, rushing on the field after he had stopped the pitcher, "do you know you are telegraphing the signs to the batters by moving around before the pitcher throws the ball?"

Bill Dahlen, formerly a shortstop on the Giants, used to shift, but he was clever enough to wait until the pitcher had started his motion, when it was too late for the batter to look at him.

Ballplayers are always looking to steal some sign so that they may "cross" the enemy. In the language of the Big-Leagues, it is "signs," never "signals." And in conclusion I reiterate my former sentiments that all is fair in love, war, and baseball except stealing signs dishonestly.

# Umpires and Close Decisions

*Ballplayers and Umpires are Regarded by the Fans as Natural Enemies, and the Fans Are about Right—Types of Arbiters and how the Players Treat them—"Silk" O'Loughlin, "Hank" O'Day, "Tim" Hurst, "Bob"" Emslie, and Others, and Close Ones they have Called—Also Some Narrow Escapes which have Followed.*

**WHEN THE** Giants were swinging through the West in 1911 on the final trip, the club played three games in Pittsburg, with the pennant at that time only a possibility more or less remote. The Pirates still had a chance, and they were fighting hard for every game, especially as they were playing on their home grounds.

The first contest of the series was on Saturday afternoon before a crowd that packed the gigantic stands which surrounded Forbes Field. The throng wanted to see the Pirates win because they were the Pirates, and the Giants beaten because they were the Giants, and were sticking their heads up above the other clubs in the race. I always think of the horse show when I play in Pittsburg, for they have the diamond horse-shoe of boxes there, you know. No; I'm wrong—it's at the Metropolitan Opera House they have the diamond horse-shoe. Anyway, the diamond horse-shoe of boxes was doing business at Forbes Field that Saturday afternoon.

This story is going to be about umpires, but the reader who has never seen the Forbes Field folks must get the atmosphere before I let the yarn into the block. Once, on a bright, sunny day there, I muffed fly after fly because the glint of Sol's rays on the diamonds blinded me.

Always now I wear smoked glasses. "Josh" Devore is so afraid that he will lose social caste when he goes to Pittsburg that he gets his finger-nails manicured before he will appear on the field. And the lady who treated him one day polished them to such an ultimate glossiness that the sun flashed on them, and he dropped two flies in left field.

"Look here, Josh," warned McGraw after the game, "I hire you to play ball and not to lead cotillions. Get some pumice stone and rub it on your finger-nails and cut out those John Drew manicures after this."

This crowd is worse after umpires than the residents of the bleachers. The game on that Saturday worked out into a pitchers' battle between Marty O'Toole, the expensive exponent of the spit ball, and "Rube" Marquard, the great left-hander. Half of "Who's Who in Pittsburg" had already split white gloves applauding when, along about the fourth or fifth inning, Fred Clarke got as far as third base with one out. The score was nothing for either side yet, and of such a delicate nature was the contest that one run was likely to decide it.

"Hans" Wagner, the peerless, and the pride of Pittsburg, was at the bat. He pushed a long fly to Murray in right field, and John caught it and threw the ball home. Clarke and the ball arrived almost simultaneously. There was a slide, a jumble of players, and a small cloud of dust blew away from the home plate.

"Ye're out!" bawled Mr. Brennan, the umpire, jerking his thumb over his shoulder with a conclusiveness that forbade argument.

Clarke jumped up and stretched his hands four feet apart, for he recognizes no conclusiveness when "one is called against him." "Safe! that much!" he shouted in Brennan's ear, showing him the four-foot margin with his hands.

There was a roar from the diamond horse-shoe that, if it could have been canned and put on a phonograph, would have made any one his fortune because it could have been turned on to accompany moving pictures of lions and other wild beasts to make them realistic.

"Say," said Clarke to Brennan, "I know a pickpocket who looks honest compared to you, and I'd rather trust my watch to a second-story worker."

Brennan was dusting off the plate and paid no attention to him. But Clarke continued to snap and bark at the umpire as he brushed himself off, referring with feeling to Mr. Brennan's immediate family, and weaving into his talk a sketch of the umpire's ancestors, for Clarke is a great master of the English language as fed to umpires.

"Mr. Clarke," said Brennan, turning at last, "you were out. Now beat it to the bench before you beat it to the clubhouse."

Clarke went grumbling and all the afternoon was after Brennan for the decision, his wrath increasing because the Pirates lost the game finally, although they would not have won it had they been given that decision. And the crowd was roaring at Brennan, too, throughout the remainder of the contest, asking him pointed questions about his habits and what his regular business was. It takes a man with nerve to make a decision like that—one that could be called either way because it was so close—and to make it as he sees it, which happened in this particular case to be against the home team.

Many times, have I, in the excitement of the moment, protested against the decision of an umpire, but fundamentally I know that the umpires are honest and are doing their best, as all ballplayers are. The umpires make mistakes and the players make errors. Many arbiters have told me that when they are working, they seldom know what inning it is or how many are out, and sometimes, in their efforts to concentrate their minds on their decisions, they say they even forget what clubs are playing and which is the home team.

The future of the game depends on the umpire, for his honesty must not be questioned. If there is a breath of suspicion against a man, he is immediately let go, because constant repetition of such a charge would result in baseball going the way of horse racing and some other sports. No scandal can creep in where the umpire is concerned, for the very popularity of baseball depends on its honesty.

"The only good umpire is a dead umpire," McGraw has declared many times when he has been disgruntled over some decision.

"I think they're all dead ones in this League," replied Devore one day, "considering the decisions that they are handing me down there at second base. Why, I had that bag by three feet and he called me out."

Many baseball fans look upon an umpire as a sort of necessary evil to the luxury of baseball, like the odor that follows an automobile.

"Kill him! He hasn't got any friends!" is an expression shouted from the stands time and again during a game.

But I know differently. I have seen umpires with friends. It is true that most ballplayers regard umpires as their natural enemies, as a boy does a schoolteacher. But "Bill" Klem has friends because I have seen him with them, and besides he has a constant companion, which is a calabash pipe.

And "Billy" Evans of the American League has lots of friends. And most all of the umpires have someone who will speak to them when they are off the field.

These men in blue travel by themselves, live at obscure hotels apart from those at which the teams stop, and slip into the ball parks unobtrusively just before game time. They never make friends with ballplayers off the field for fear that there might be a hint of scandal. Seldom do they take the same train with a club unless it cannot be avoided.

Billy Evans, Umpire

"Hank" O'Day, the veteran of the National League staff, and Brennan took the same train out of Chicago with the Giants in the fall of 1911 because we stopped in Pittsburg for one game, and they had to be there to umpire. It was the only available means of transportation. But they stayed by themselves in another Pullman until someone told them "Charley" Faust, the official jinx-killer of the Giants, was doing his stunt. Then they both came back into the Giants' car and for the first time in my life I saw "Hank" O'Day laugh. His face acted as if it wasn't accustomed to the exercise and broke all in funny new wrinkles, like a glove when you put it on for the first time.

There are several types of umpires, and ballplayers are always studying the species to find out the best way to treat each man to get the most out of him. There are autocrats and stubborn ones and good fellows and weak-kneed ones, almost as many kinds as there are human beings. The autocrat of the umpire world is "Silk" O'Loughlin, now appearing with a rival show.

"Hank" O'Day, Umpire

"There are no close plays," says "Silk." "A man is always out or safe, or it is a ball or a strike, and the umpire, if he is a good man and knows his business, is always right. For instance, I am always right."

He refuses to let the players discuss a decision with him, maintaining that there is never any room for argument. If a man makes any talk with him, it is quick to the shower bath. "Silk" has a voice of which he is proud and declares that he shares the honors with Caruso and that it is only his profession as an umpire that keeps him off the grand-opera circuit. I have heard a lot of American League ballplayers say at various times that they wished he was on the grand-opera circuit or some more calorific circuit, but they were mostly prejudiced at those moments by some sentiments which "Silk" had just voiced in an official capacity.

As is well known in baseball, "Silk" is the inventor of "Strike Tuh!" and the creased trousers for umpires. I have heard American League players declare that they are afraid to slide when "Silk" is close down over a play for fear they will bump up against his trousers and cut themselves. He is one of the kind of umpires who can go through a game on the hottest summer day, running about the bases, and still keep his collar unwilted. At the end he will look as if he were dressed for an afternoon tea.

"Silk" O'Loughlin, Umpire

Always he wears on his right hand, which is his salary or decision wing, a large diamond that sparkles in the sunlight every time he calls a man out. Many American League players assert that he would rather call a man out than safe, so that he can shimmer his "cracked ice," but again they are usually influenced by circumstances. Such is "Silk," well named.

Corresponding to him in the National League is "Billy" Klem. He always wears a Norfolk jacket because he thinks it more stylish, and perhaps it is, and he refuses to don a wind pad. Ever notice him working behind the bat? But I am going to let you in on a secret. That chest is not all his own. Beneath his jacket he carries his armor, a protector, and under his trousers' legs are shin guards. He insists that all players call him "Mr." He says that he thinks maybe soon his name will be in the social register. "Larry" Doyle thought that he had received the raw end of a decision at second base one day.

"Bill" Klem, Umpire

He ran down to first, where Klem had retreated after he passed his judgment. "Say, 'Bill,'" exploded "Larry," "that man didn't touch the bag—didn't come within six feet of it."

"Say, Doyle," replied Klem, "when you talk to me call me 'Mr. Klem.'"

"But, Mr. Klem—" amended "Larry."

Klem hurriedly drew a line with his foot as Doyle approached him menacingly. "But if you come over that line, you're out of the game, Mr. Doyle," he threatened.

"All right," answered "Larry," letting his pugilistic attitude evaporate before the abruptness of Klem as the mist does before the classic noonday sun, "but, Mr. Klem, I only wanted to ask you if that clock in center field is right by your watch, because I know everything about you is right."

"Larry" went back, grinning and considering that he had put one over on Klem—Mr. Klem.

For a long time "Johnny" Evers of the Chicago club declared that Klem owed him $5 on a bet he had lost to the second baseman and had neglected to pay. Now John, when he was right, could make almost any umpirical goat leap from crag to crag and do somersaults en route. He kept pestering Klem about that measly $5 bet, not in an obtrusive way, you understand, but by such delicate methods as holding up five fingers when Klem glanced down on the coaching lines where he was stationed, or by writing a large "5" in the dirt at the home plate with the butt of his bat as he came up when Klem was umpiring on balls and strikes, or by counting slowly and casually up to five and stopping with an abruptness that could not be misconstrued.

One day John let his temper get away from him and bawled Klem out in his most approved fashion.

"Here's your five, Mr. Evers," said Klem, handing him a five-dollar bill, "and now you are fined $25."

"And it was worth it," answered Evers, "to bawl you out."

Next comes the O'Day type, and there is only one of them, "Hank." He is the stubborn kind—or perhaps *was* the stubborn kind, would be better, as he is now a manager. He is bull-headed. If a manager gets after him for a decision, he is likely to go up in the air and, not meaning to do it, call close ones against the club that has made the kick, for it must be remembered that umpires are only "poor weak mortals after all." O'Day has to be handled with shock absorbers. McGraw tries to do it, but shock absorbers do not fit him well, and the first thing that usually occurs is a row.

"Let me do the kicking, boys," McGraw always warns his players before a contest that O'Day is going to umpire.

He does not want to see any of his men put out of the game.

"Bill" Dahlen always got on O'Day's nerves by calling him "Henry." For some reason, O'Day does not like the name, and "Bill" Dahlen discovered long ago the most irritating inflection to give it so that it would rasp on O'Day's ears. He does not mind "Hank" and is not a "Mister" umpire. But every time Dahlen would call O'Day "Henry" it was the cold shower and the civilian's clothes for his.

Dahlen was playing in St. Louis many years ago when the racetrack was right opposite the ballpark. "Bill" had a preference in one of the later races one day and was anxious to get across the street and make a little bet. He had obtained a leave of absence on two preceding days by calling O'Day "Henry" and had lost money on the horses he had selected as fleet of foot. But this last time he had a "sure thing" and was banking on some positive information which had been slipped to him by a friend of the friend of the man who owned the winner, and "Bill" wanted to be there.

Along about the fifth inning, "Bill" figured that it was time for him to get a start, so he walked up to O'Day and said: "Henry, do you know who won the first race?"

"No, and you won't either, Mr. Dahlen," answered "Hank." "You are fined $25, and you stay here and play the game out."

Someone had tipped "Hank" off. And the saddest part of the story is that "Bill's" horse walked home, and he could not get a bet down on him. "First time it ever failed to work," groaned "Bill" in the hotel that night, "and I said 'Henry' in my meanest way, too."

Most clubs try to keep an umpire from feeling hostile toward the team because, even if he means to see a play right, he is likely to call a close one against his enemies, not intending to be dishonest. It would simply mean that you would not get any close ones from him, and the close ones count. Some umpires can be reasoned with, and a good fair protest will often make a man think perhaps he has called it wrong, and he will give you the edge on the next decision. A player must understand an umpire to know how to approach him to the best advantage. O'Day cannot be reasoned with. It is as dangerous to argue with him as it is to try to ascertain how much gasoline is in the tank of an automobile by sticking down the lighted end of a cigar or a cigarette.

Emslie will listen to a reasonable argument. He is one of the finest umpires that ever broke into the League, I think. He is a good fellow. Far be it from me to be disloyal to my manager, for I think that he is the greatest that ever won a pennant, but Emslie put one over on McGraw in 1911 when it was being said that Emslie was getting so old he could not see a play.

Bob Emslie, Umpire

"I'll bet," said McGraw to him one day after he had called one against the Giants, "that I can put a baseball and an orange on second base, and you can't tell the difference standing at the home plate, Bob."

Emslie made no reply right then, but when the eye test for umpires was established by Mr. Lynch, the president of the League, "Bob" passed it at the head of the list and then turned around and went up to Chatham in Ontario, Canada, and made a high score with the rifle in a shooting match up there. After he had done that, he was umpiring at the Polo Grounds one day.

"Want to take me on for a shooting go, John?" he asked McGraw as he passed him.

"No, Bob, you're all right. I give it to you," answered McGraw, who had long forgotten his slur on Emslie's eyesight.

Emslie is the sort of umpire who rules by the bond of good fellowship rather than by the voice of authority. "Old Bob" has one "groove" and it is a personal matter about which he is very sensitive. He is under cover. It is no secret, or I would not give way on him. But that luxuriant growth of hair, apparent, comes off at night like his collar and necktie. It used to be quite the fad in the League to "josh" "Bob" about his wig, but that pastime has sort of died out now because he has proven himself to be such a good fellow.

I had to laugh to myself, and not boisterously, in the season of 1911 when Mr. Lynch appointed "Jack" Doyle, formerly a first baseman and a hot-headed player, an umpire and scheduled him to work with Emslie. I remembered the time several seasons ago when Doyle took offence at one of "Bob's" decisions and wrestled him all over the infield trying to get his wig off and show him up before the crowd. And then Emslie and he worked together like Damon and Pythias. This business makes strange bed-fellows.

Emslie was umpiring in New York one day in the season of 1909, when the Giants were playing St. Louis. A wild pitch hit Emslie over the heart and he wilted down, unconscious. The players gathered around him, and Bresnahan, who was catching for St. Louis at the time, started to help "Bob." Suddenly the old umpire came to and began to fight off his first-aid-to-the-injured corps. No one could understand his attitude as he struggled to his feet and strolled away by himself, staggering a little and apparently dizzy. At last, he came back and gamely finished the business of the day. I never knew why he fought with the men who were trying to help him until several weeks later, when we were playing in Pittsburg. As I came out from under the stand on my way to the bench, Emslie happened to be making his entrance at the same time.

"Say, Matty," he asked me, "that time in New York did my wig come off? Did Bresnahan take my wig off?"

"No, Bob," I replied, "he was only trying to help you."

"I thought maybe he took it off while I was down and out and showed me up before the crowd," he apologized.

"Listen, Bob," I said. "I don't believe there is a player in either League who would do that, and, if any youngster tried it now, he would probably be licked."

"I'm glad to hear you say that, Matty," answered the old man, as he picked up his wind pad and prepared to go to work.

And he called more bad ones on me that day than he ever had in his life before, but I never mentioned the wig to him.

Most umpires declare they have off days just like players, when they know that they are making mistakes and cannot help it. If a pitcher of Mordecai Brown's kind, who depends largely on his control for his effectiveness, happens to run up against an umpire with a bad day, he might just as well go back to the bench. Brown is a great man to work the corners of the plate, and if the umpire is missing strikes, he is forced to lay the ball over and then the batters whang it out. Johnstone had an off day in Chicago in 1911, when Brown was working.

"What's the use of my tryin' to pitch, Jim," said Brown, throwing down his glove and walking to the bench disgusted, "if you don't know a strike when you see one?"

Sometimes an umpire who has been good will go into a long slump when he cannot call things right and knows it. Men like that get as discouraged as a pitcher who goes bad. There used to be one in the National League who was a pretty fair umpire when he started and seemed to be getting along fine until he hit one of those slumps. Then he began calling everything wrong and knew it. At last, he quit, and the next time I saw him was in Philadelphia in the 1911 world's series. He was a policeman.

"Hello, Matty," he shouted at me as we were going into Shibe Park for the first game there. "I can call you by your first name now," and he waved his hand real friendly.

The last conversation I had with that fellow, unless my recollection fails me entirely, was anything but friendly.

Umpires have told me that sometimes they see a play one way and call it another, and, as soon as the decision is announced, they realize that they have called it wrong. This malady has put more than one umpire out. A man on the National League staff has informed me since, that he called a hit fair that was palpably two feet foul in one of the most important games ever played in baseball, when he saw the ball strike on foul ground.

"I couldn't help saying 'Fair ball,'" declared this man, and he is one of the best in the National League. "Luckily," he added, "the team against which the decision went won the game."

Many players assert that arbiters hold a personal grudge against certain men who have put up too strenuous kicks, and for that reason the wise ones are careful how

Fred Tenney, New York Giants

they talk to umpires of this sort. Fred Tenney has said for a long time that Mr. Klem gives him a shade the worst of it on all close ones because he had a run in with that umpire one day when they came to blows. Tenney is a great man to pick out the good ones when at the bat, and Fred says that if he is up with a three and two count on him now, Klem is likely to call the next one a strike if it is close, not because he is dishonest, but because he has a certain personal prejudice which he cannot overcome. And the funny part about it is that Tenney does not hold this up against Klem.

Humorous incidents are always occurring in connection with umpires. We were playing in Boston one day a few years ago, and the score was 3 to 0 against the Giants in the ninth inning. Becker knocked a home run with two men on the bases, and it tied the count. With men on first and third bases and one out in the last half of the ninth, a Boston batter tapped one to Merkle which I thought he trapped, but Johnstone, the umpire, said he caught it on the fly. It was simplicity itself to double the runner up off first base who also thought Merkle had trapped the ball and had started for second. That retired the side, and we won the game in the twelfth inning, whereas Boston would have taken it in the ninth if Johnstone had said the ball was trapped instead of caught on the fly.

It was a very hot day, and those extra three innings in the box knocked me out. I was sick for a week with stomach trouble afterwards and could not pitch in Chicago, where we made our next stop. That was a case of where a decision in my favor "made me sick."

"Tim" Hurst, the old American League umpire, was one of the most picturesque judges that ever spun an indicator. He was the sort who would take a player at his word and fight him blow for blow. "Tim" was umpiring in Baltimore in the old days when there was a runner on first base.

"The man started to steal," says Tim. He was telling the story only the other day in McGraw's billiard room in New York, and it is better every time he does it. "As he left the bag, he spiked the first baseman and that player attempted to trip him. The second baseman blocked the runner and, in sliding into the bag, the latter tried to spike 'Hugh' Jennings, who was playing shortstop and covering, while Jennings sat on him to knock the wind

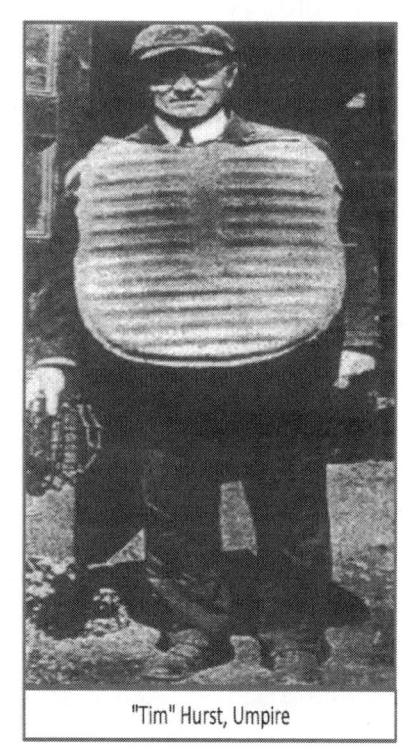

"Tim" Hurst, Umpire

out. The batter hit Robinson, who was catching, on the hands with his bat so that he couldn't throw, and 'Robbie' trod on my toes with his spikes and shoved his glove into my face so that I couldn't see to give the decision. It was one of the hardest that I have ever been called upon to make."

"What did you do?" I asked him.

"I punched 'Robbie' in the ribs, called it a foul and sent the runner back," replied "Tim."

# The Game that Cost a Pennant

*The Championship of the National League was Decided in 1908 in One Game between the Giants and Cubs—Few Fans Know that it Was Mr. Brush who Induced the Disgruntled New York Players to Meet Chicago—This is the "Inside" Story of the Famous Game, Including "Fred" Merkle's Part in the Series of Events which Led up to it.*

**THE NEW** York Giants and the Chicago Cubs played a game at the Polo Grounds on October 8, 1908, which decided the championship of the National League in one afternoon, which was responsible for the deaths of two spectators, who fell from the elevated railroad structure overlooking the grounds, which made Fred Merkle famous for not touching second, which caused lifelong friends to become bitter enemies, and which, altogether, was the most dramatic and important contest in the history of baseball. It stands out from every-day events like the battle of Waterloo and the assassination of President Lincoln. It was a baseball

Fred Merkle, New York Giants

tragedy from a New York point of view. The Cubs won by the score of 4 to 2.

Behind this game is some "inside" history that has never been written. Few persons, outside of the members of the New York club, know that it was only after a great deal of consultation the game was finally played, only after the urging of John T. Brush, the president of the club. The Giants were risking, in one afternoon, their chances of winning the pennant and the world's series—the concentration of their hopes of a season—because the Cubs claimed the right on a technicality to play this one game for the championship. Many members of the New York club felt that it would be fighting for what they had already won, as did their supporters. This made bad feeling between the teams and between the spectators, until the whole dramatic situation leading up to the famous game culminated in the climax of that afternoon. The nerves of the players were rasped raw with the strain, and the town wore a fringe of nervous prostration. It all burst forth in the game.

Among other things, Frank Chance, the manager of the Cubs, had a cartilage in his neck broken when some rooter hit him with a handy pop bottle, several spectators hurt one another when they switched from conversational to fistic arguments, large portions of the fence at the Polo Grounds were broken down by patrons who insisted on gaining entrance, and most of the police of New York were present to keep order. They had their clubs unlimbered, too, acting more as if on strike duty than restraining the spectators at a pleasure park. Last of all, that night, after we had lost the game, the report filtered through New York that Fred Merkle, then a youngster and around whom the whole situation revolved, had committed suicide. Of course it was not true, for Merkle is one of the gamest ballplayers that ever lived.

My part in the game was small. I started to pitch and I didn't finish. The Cubs beat me because I never had less on the ball in my life. What I can't understand to this day is why it took them so long to hit me. Frequently it has been said that "Cy" Seymour started the Cubs on their victorious way and lost the game, because he misjudged a long hit jostled to center field by "Joe" Tinker at the beginning of the third inning, in which chapter they made four runs. The hit went for three bases.

Seymour, playing center field, had a bad background against which to judge fly balls that afternoon, facing the shadows of the towering stand, with the uncertain horizon formed by persons perched on the roof. A baseball writer has said that, when Tinker came to the bat in that fatal inning, I turned in the box and motioned Seymour back, and instead of obeying instructions he crept a few steps closer to the infield. I don't recall giving any advice to "Cy," as he knew the Chicago batters as well as I did and how to play for them.

Tinker, with his long bat, swung on a ball intended to be a low curve over the outside corner of the plate, but it failed to break well. He pushed out a high fly to center field, and I turned with the ball to see Seymour take a couple of steps toward the diamond, evidently thinking it would drop somewhere behind second base. He appeared to be uncertain in his judgment of the hit until he suddenly turned and started to run back. That must have been when the ball cleared the roof of the stand and was visible above the skyline. He ran wildly. Once he turned, and then ran on again, at last sticking up his hands and having the ball fall just beyond them. He chased it and picked it up, but Tinker had reached third base by that time. If he had let the ball roll into the crowd in center field, the Cub could have made only two bases on the hit, according to the ground rules. That was a mistake, but it made little difference in the end.

All the players, both the Cubs and the Giants, were under a terrific strain that day, and Seymour, in his anxiety to be sure to catch the ball, misjudged it. Did you ever stand out in the field at a ball park with thirty thousand crazy, shouting fans looking at you and watch a ball climb and climb into the air and have to make up your mind exactly where it is going to land and then have to be there, when it arrived, to greet it, realizing all the time that if you are not there you are going to be everlastingly roasted? It is no cure for nervous diseases, that situation. Probably forty-nine times out of fifty Seymour would have caught the fly.

"I misjudged that ball," said "Cy" to me in the clubhouse after the game. "I'll take the blame for it."

He accepted all the abuse the newspapers handed him without a murmur and I don't think myself that it was more than an incident in the game. I'll try to show later in this story where the real "break" came.

Just one mistake, made by "Fred" Merkle, resulted in this play-off game. Several newspaper men have called September 23, 1908, "Merkle Day," because it was on that day he ran to the clubhouse from first base instead of by way of second, when "Al" Bridwell whacked out the hit that apparently won the game from the Cubs. Any other player on the team would have undoubtedly done the same thing under the circumstances, as the custom had been in vogue all around the circuit during the season. It was simply Fred Merkle's misfortune to have been on first base at the critical moment.

"Al" Bridwell, Chicago Cubs

The situation which gave rise to the incident is well known to every follower of baseball. Merkle, as a pinch hitter, had singled with two out in the ninth inning and the score tied, sending McCormick from first base to third. "Al" Bridwell came up to the bat and smashed a single to center field. McCormick crossed the plate, and that, according to the customs of the League, ended the game, so Merkle dug for the clubhouse. Evers and Tinker ran through the crowd which had flocked on the field and got the ball, touching second and claiming that Merkle had been forced out there.

Most of the spectators did not understand the play, as Merkle was under the shower bath when the alleged put-out was made, but they started after "Hank" O'Day, the umpire, to be on the safe side. He made a speedy departure under the grand-stand and the crowd got the put-out unassisted. Finally, while somewhere near Coogan's Bluff, he called Merkle out and the score a tie. When the boys heard this in the clubhouse, they laughed, for it didn't seem like a situation to be taken seriously. But it turned out to be one of those things that the farther it goes the more serious it becomes.

Fred Merkle, New York Giants shown leading off first base held by Frank Chance of the Chicago Cubs

"Connie" Mack, the manager of the Athletics, says: "There is no luck in Big-League baseball. In a schedule of one hundred and fifty-four games, the lucky and unlucky plays break about even, except in the matter of injuries." But Mack's theory does not include a schedule of one hundred and fifty-five games, with the result depending on the one hundred and fifty-fifth. Chicago had a lot of injured athletes early in the season of 1908, and the Giants had shot out ahead in the race in grand style. In the meantime, the Cubs' cripples began to recuperate, and that lamentable event on September 23 seemed to be the turning-point in the Giants' fortunes.

Almost within a week afterwards, Bresnahan had an attack of sciatic rheumatism and "Mike" Donlin was limping about the outfield, leading a great case of "Charley horse." Tenney was bandaged from his waist down and should have been wearing crutches instead of playing first base on a Big-League club. Doyle was badly spiked and in the hospital.

"Mike" Donlin, New York Giants

McGraw's daily greeting to his athletes when he came to the park was: "How are the cripples? Any more to add to the list of identified dead to-day?"

Merkle moped. He lost flesh, and time after time begged McGraw to send him to a minor league or to turn him loose altogether. "It wasn't your fault," was the regular response of the manager who makes it a habit to stand by his men.

We played on with the cripples, many double-headers costing the pitchers extra effort, and McGraw not daring to take a chance on losing a game if there were any opportunity to win it. He could not rest any of his men.

Merkle lost weight and seldom spoke to the other players as the Cubs crept up on us day after day and more men were hurt. He felt that he was responsible for this change in the luck of the club. None of the players felt this way toward him, and many tried to cheer him up, but he was inconsolable. The team went over to Philadelphia, and Coveleski, the pitcher we later drove out of the League, beat us three times, winning the last game by the scantiest of margins. The result of that series left us three to play with Boston to tie the Cubs if they won from Pittsburg the next day, Sunday. If the Pirates had taken that Sunday game, it would have given them the pennant. We returned to New York on Saturday night very much downhearted.

"Lose me. I'm the jinx," Merkle begged McGraw that night.

"You stick," replied the manager.

While we had been losing, the Cubs had been coming fast. It seemed as if they could not drop a game. At last Cincinnati beat them one, which was the only thing that made the famous season tie possible. There is an interesting anecdote connected with that Cincinnati contest which goes to prove the honesty of baseball.

Two of the closest friends in the game are "Hans" Lobert, then with

"Hans" Lobert, Cincinnati Reds

the Reds, and Overall, the former Chicago pitcher. It looked as if Chicago had the important game won up to the ninth inning when Lobert came to the bat with two men out and two on the bases. Here he had a chance to overcome the lead of one run which the Cubs had gained, and win the contest for the home club, but he would beat his best friend and maybe put the Cubs out of the running for the pennant.

Lobert had two balls and two strikes when he smashed the next pitch to center field, scoring both the base runners. The hit came near beating the Cubs out of the championship. It would have if we had taken one of those close games against Philadelphia. Lobert was broken-hearted over his hit, for he wanted the Cubs to win. On his way to the clubhouse, he walked with Overall, the two-striding side by side like a couple of mourners.

Orval Overall, Chicago Cubs

"I'm sorry, 'Orvie,'" said Lobert. "I would not have made that hit for my year's salary if I could have helped it."

"That's all right, 'Hans,'" returned Overall. "It's all part of the game."

Next came the famous game in Chicago on Sunday between the Cubs and the Pittsburg Pirates, when a victory for the latter club would have meant the pennant and the big game would never have been played. Ten thousand persons crowded into the Polo Grounds that Sunday afternoon and watched a little electric score board which showed the plays as made in Chicago. For the first time in my life, I heard a New York crowd cheering the Cubs with great fervor, for on their victory hung our only chances of ultimate success. The same man who was shouting himself hoarse for the Cubs that afternoon was for taking a vote on the desirability of poisoning the whole Chicago team on the following Thursday. Even the New York players were rooting for the Cubs.

The Chicago team at last won the game when Clarke was called out at third base on a close play, late in the contest. With the decision, the Pirates' last chance went glimmering. The Giants now had three games to win from Boston on Monday, Tuesday and Wednesday, to make the deciding game on Thursday necessary. We won those, and the stage was cleared for the big number.

The National Commission gave the New York club the option of playing three games out of five for the championship or risking it all on one contest. As more than half of the club was tottering on the brink of the hospital, it was decided that all hope should be hung on one game. By this time, Merkle had lost twenty pounds, and his eyes were hollow and his cheeks sunken. The newspapers showed him no mercy, and the fans never failed to criticize and hiss him when he appeared on the field. He stuck to it and showed up in the ballpark every day, putting on his uniform and practicing. It was a game thing to do. A lot of men, under the same fire, would have quit cold. McGraw was with him all the way.

But it was not until after considerable discussion that it was decided to play that game. All the men felt disgruntled because they believed they would be playing for something they had already won.

Even McGraw was so wrought up, he said in the clubhouse the night before the game: "I don't care whether you fellows play this game or not. You can take a vote."

A vote was taken, and the players were not unanimous, some protesting it ought to be put up to the League directors so that, if they wanted to rob the team of a pennant, they would have to take the blame. Others insisted it would look like quitting, and it was finally decided to appoint a committee to call upon Mr. Brush, the president of the club, who was ill in bed in the Lambs club at the time. Devlin, Bresnahan, Donlin, Tenney, and I were on that committee.

Art Devlin, New York Giants

"Mr. Brush," I said to my employer, having been appointed the spokesman, "McGraw has left it up to us to decide whether we shall meet the Chicago team for the championship of the National League to-morrow. A lot of the boys do not believe we ought to be forced to play over again for something we have already won, so the players have appointed this committee of five to consult with you and get your opinion on the subject. What we decide goes with them."

Mr. Brush looked surprised. I was nervous, more so than when I am in the box with three on the bases and "Joe" Tinker at the bat. Bresnahan fumbled with his hat, and Devlin coughed. Tenney leaned more heavily on his cane, and Donlin blew his nose. We five big athletes were embarrassed in the presence of this sick man. Suddenly it struck us all at the same time that the game would have to be played to keep ourselves square with our own ideas of courage. Even if the Cubs had claimed it on a technicality, even if we had really won the pennant once, that game had to be played now. We all saw that, and it was this thin, ill man in bed who made us see it even before he had said a word. It was the expression on his face.

It seemed to say, "And I had confidence in you, boys, to do the right thing." "I'm going to leave it to you," he answered "You boys can play the game or put it up to the directors of the League to decide as you want. But I shouldn't think you would stop now after making all this fight."

The committee called an executive session, and we all thought of the crowd of fans looking forward to the game and of what the newspapers would say if we refused to play it and of Mr. Brush lying there, the man who wanted us to play, and it was rapidly and unanimously decided to imitate "Steve" Brodie and take a chance.

"We'll play," I said to Mr. Brush.

"I'm glad," he answered. "And, say, boys," he added, as we started to file out, "I want to tell you something. Win or lose, I'm going to give the players a bonus of $10,000."

That night was a wild one in New York. The air crackled with excitement and baseball. I went home but couldn't sleep for I live near the Polo Grounds, and the crowd began to gather there early in the evening of the day before the game to be ready for the opening of the gates the next morning. They tooted horns all night and were never still.

When I reported at the ballpark, the gates had been closed by order of the National Commission, but the streets for blocks around the Polo Grounds were jammed with persons fighting to get to the entrances.

The players in the clubhouse had little to say to one another, but, after the bandages were adjusted, McGraw called his men around him and said: "Chance will probably pitch Pfiester or Brown. If Pfiester works there is no use trying to steal. He won't give you any lead. The right-handed batters ought to wait him out and the left-handers hit him when he gets in a hole. Matty is going to pitch for us."

Pfiester is a left-hand pitcher who watches the bases closely.

Merkle had reported at the clubhouse as usual and had put on his uniform. He hung on the edge of the group as McGraw spoke, and then we all went to the field. It was hard for us to play that game with the crowd, which was there, but harder for the Cubs. In one place, the fence was broken down, and some employees were playing a stream of water from a fire hose on the cavity to keep the crowd back. Many preferred a ducking to missing the game and ran through the stream to the lines around the field. A string of fans recklessly straddled the roof of the old grand-stand.

Jack Pfeister, Chicago Cubs

Every once in a while some group would break through the restraining ropes and scurry across the diamond to what appeared to be a better point of vantage. This would let a throng loose which hurried one way and another and mixed in with the players. More police had to be summoned. As I watched that half-wild multitude before the contest, I could think of three or four things I would rather do than umpire the game.

I had rested my arm four days, not having pitched in the Boston series, and I felt that it should be in pretty good condition. Before that respite, I had been in nine out of fifteen games. But as I started to warm up, the ball refused to break. I couldn't get anything on it.

"What's the matter, Rog?" I asked Bresnahan. "They won't break for me."

"It'll come as you start to work," he replied, although I could see that he, too, was worried.

John M. Ward, the old ball-player and now one of the owners of the Boston National League club, has told me since that, after working almost every day as I had been doing, it does a pitcher's arm no good to lay off for three or four days. Only a week or ten days will accomplish any results. It would have been better for me to continue to work as often as I had been doing, for the short rest only seemed to deaden my arm.

The crowd that day was inflammable. The players caught this incendiary spirit. McGinnity, batting out to our infield in practice, insisted on driving Chance away from the plate before the Cubs' leader thought his team had had its full share of the batting rehearsal. "Joe" shoved him a little, and in a minute, fists were flying, although Chance and McGinnity are very good friends off the field. Fights immediately started all around in the stands. I remember seeing two men roll from the top to the bottom of the right-field bleachers, over the heads of the rest of the spectators. And they were yanked to their feet and run out of the park by the police.

"Too bad," I said to Bresnahan, nodding my head toward the departing belligerents, "they couldn't have waited until they saw the game, anyway. I'll bet they stood outside the park all night to get in, only to be run out before it started."

I forgot the crowd, forgot the fights, and didn't hear the howling after the game started. I knew only one thing, and that was my curved ball wouldn't break for me. It surprised me that the Cubs didn't hit it far, right away, but two of them fanned in the first inning and Herzog threw out Evers. Then came our first time at bat. Pfiester was plainly nervous and hit Tenney. Herzog walked and Bresnahan fanned out, Herzog being doubled up at second because he tried to advance on a short, passed ball. "Mike" Donlin whisked a double to right field and Tenney counted.

For the first time in almost a month, Merkle smiled. He was drawn up in the corner of the bench, pulling away from the rest of us as if he had some contagious disease and was quarantined. For a minute it looked as if we had them going. Chance yanked Pfiester out of the box with him protesting that he had been robbed on the decisions on balls and strikes. Brown was brought into the game and fanned Devlin. That ended the inning.

We never had a chance against Brown. His curve was breaking sharply, and his control was microscopic. We went back to the field in the second with that one run lead. Chance made the first hit of the game off me in the second, but I caught him sleeping at first base, according to Klem's decision. There was a kick, and Hofman, joining in the chorus of protests, was sent to the clubhouse.

Tinker started the third with that memorable triple which gave the Cubs their chance. I couldn't make my curve break.

I didn't have anything on the ball. "Rog," I said to Bresnahan, "I haven't got anything to-day."

"Keep at it, Matty," he replied. "We'll get them all right."

I looked in at the bench, and McGraw signaled me to go on pitching. Kling singled and scored Tinker. Brown sacrificed, sending Kling to second, and Sheckard flied out to Seymour, Kling being held on second base. I lost Evers, because I was afraid to put the ball over the plate for him, and he walked. Two were out now, and we had yet a chance to win the game as the score was only tied. But Schulte doubled, and Kling scored, leaving men on second and third bases. Still, we had a Mongolian's chance with

Jimmy Sheckard, Chicago Cubs

them only one run ahead of us. Frank Chance, with his under jaw set like the fender on a trolley car, caught a curved ball over the inside corner of the plate and pushed it to right field for two bases. That was the most remarkable batting performance I have ever witnessed since I have been in the Big-Leagues. A right-handed hitter naturally slaps a ball over the outside edge of the plate to right field, but Chance pushed this one, on the inside, with the handle of his bat, just over Tenney's hands and on into the crowd. The hit scored Evers and Schulte and dissolved the game right there. It was the "break." Steinfeldt fanned.

Harry Steinfeldt, Chicago Cubs

None of the players spoke to one another as they went to the bench. Even McGraw was silent. We knew it was gone. Merkle was drawn up behind the water cooler. Once he said: "It was my fault, boys."

No one answered him. Inning after inning, our batters were mowed down by the great pitching of Brown, who was never better. His control of his curved ball was marvelous, and he had all his speed. As the innings dragged by, the spectators lost heart, and the cowbells ceased to jingle, and the cheering lost its resonant ring. It was now a surly growl.

Then the seventh! We had our one glimmer of sunshine. Devlin started with a single to center, and McCormick shoved a drive to right field. Recalling that Bridwell was more or less of a pinch hitter, Brown passed him purposely and Doyle was sent to the bat in my place.

As he hobbled to the plate on his weak foot, said McGraw: "Hit one, Larry."

The crowd broke into cheers again and was stamping its feet. The bases were full, and no one was out. Then Doyle popped up a weak foul behind the catcher. His batting eye was dim and rusty through long disuse. Kling went back for it, and someone threw a pop bottle which narrowly missed him, and another scaled a cushion. But Kling kept on and got what he went after, which was the ball. He has a habit of doing that. Tenney flied to Schulte, counting Devlin on the catch, and Tinker threw out Herzog. The game was gone. Never again did we have a chance.

Frank Schulte, Chicago Cubs

It was a glum lot of players in the clubhouse.

Merkle came up to McGraw and said: "Mac, I've lost you one pennant. Fire me before I can do any more harm."

"Fire you?" replied McGraw. "We ran the wrong way of the track to-day. That's all. Next year is another season, and do you think I'm going to let you go after the gameness you've shown through all this abuse? Why you're the kind of a guy I've been lookin' for many years. I could use a carload like you. Forget this season and come around next spring. The newspapers will have forgotten it all then. Good-by, boys." And he slipped out of the clubhouse.

"He's a regular guy," said Merkle.

Merkle has lived down that failure to touch second and proved himself to be one of the gamest players that ever stood in a diamond. Many times, since has he vindicated himself. He is a great first baseman now, and McGraw and he are close friends. That is the "inside" story of the most important game ever played in baseball and Merkle's connection with it.

# When the Teams Are in Spring Training

*The Hardships of the Preliminary Practice in Limbering up Muscles and Reducing Weight for the Big Campaign—How a Ball Club is Whipped into Playing Shape—Trips to the South Not the Picnics they Seem to Be—The Battle of the Bushers to Stay in the Big Show—Making a Pitcher—Some Fun on the Side, including the Adventure of the Turkish Bath.*

**SPRING TRAINING!** The words probably remind the reader of the sunny South and light exercise and good food and rubs and other luxuries, but the reader perhaps has never been with a Big-League ballclub when it is getting ready to go into a six months' campaign.
All I can ever remember after a training trip is taking off and putting on a uniform and running around the ballpark under the inspiration of John McGraw, and he is some inspirer.

The heavier a man gets through the winter, the harder the routine work is for him, and a few years ago I almost broke down and cried out of sympathy for Otis Crandall, who arrived in camp very corpulent.

"What have you been doing this winter, Otie?" McGraw asked him after shaking hands in greeting, "appearing with a show as the stout lady? You'll have to take a lot of that off."

"Taking it off" meant running several miles every day so bundled up that the Indiana agriculturist looked like the pictures published of "Old Doc" Cook which showed him discovering the north pole. Ever since, Crandall's spring training, like charity, has begun at home, and he takes exercise night and morning throughout the winter, so that when he comes into camp his weight will be somewhere near normal. In 1911 he had the best year of his career. He is the type of man who cannot afford to carry too much weight. He is stronger when he is slimmer.

In contrast to him is George Wiltse, who maps out a training course with the idea of adding several pounds, as he is better with all the real weight he can put on. By that I do not mean any fat.

George came whirling and spinning and waltzing and turkey-trotting and pirouetting across the field at Marlin Springs, Texas, the Giants' spring training headquarters, one day in the spring of 1911, developing steps that would have ruled him off any cotillion floor in New York in the days of the ban on the grizzly bear and kindred dances. Suddenly he dove down with his left hand and reached as far as he could.

"What's that one, George?" I yelled as he passed me.

"Getting ready to cover first base on a slow hit, Matty," he replied, and was off on another series of hand springs that made him look more like a contortionist rehearsing for an act which he was going to take out for the "big time" than a ball-player getting ready for the season.

But perhaps some close followers of baseball statistics will recall a game that Wiltse took from the Cubs in 1911 by a wonderful one-hand reaching catch of a low throw to first base. Two Chicago runners were on the bags at the time and the loss of that throw would have meant that they both scored. Wiltse caught the ball, and it made the third out, and the Giants won the game.

Thousands of fans applauded the catch, but the play was not the result of the exigencies of the moment. It was the outcome of forethought used months before.

Spectators at ball games who wonder at the marvelous fielding of Wiltse should watch him getting ready during the spring season at Marlin. He is a tireless worker, and when he is not pitching, he is doing handsprings and other acrobatic acts to limber up all his muscles. It is torture then, but it pays in the end.

When I was a young fellow and read about the Big-League clubs going South, I used to think what a grand life that must be. Riding in Pullmans, some pleasant exercise which did not entail the responsibility of a ball game, and plenty of food, with a little social recreation, were all parts of my dream. A young ball-player looks on his first spring training trip as a stage-struck young woman regards the theatre. She cannot wait for her first rehearsal, and she thinks only of the lobster suppers and the applause and the lights and the life, but nowhere in her dream is there a place for the raucous voice of the stage manager and the long jumps of "one-night stands" with the loss of sleep and the poor meals and the cold dressing rooms. As actors begin to dread the drudgery of rehearsing, so do baseball men detest the drill of the spring training. The only thing that I can think of right away which is more tiresome and less interesting is signal practice with a college football team.

About the time that the sap starts up in the trees and the young man's fancy lightly turns to thoughts of love and baseball, the big trek starts. Five hundred ballplayers, attached more or less firmly to sixteen major league clubs, spread themselves out over the southern part of the United States, from Florida to California, and begin to prepare for the campaign that is to furnish the answer to that annual question, "Which is the best baseball club in the world?"

In the case of the Giants, McGraw, with a flock of youngsters, has already arrived when the older men begin to drift into camp. The youngsters, who have come from the bushes and realize that this is their one big chance to make good, to be a success or a failure in their chosen profession—in short, to become a Big-Leaguer or go back to the bushes for good—have already been working for ten days and are in fair shape.

They stare at the regulars as the veterans straggle in by twos and threes, and McGraw has a brief greeting for each. He could use a rubber stamp.

"How are you, Matty? What kind of shape are you in? Let's see you in a uniform at nine o'clock to-morrow morning."

When I first start South, for the spring trip, after shivering through a New York winter, I arouse myself to some enthusiasm over the prospect, but all this has evaporated after listening to that terse speech from McGraw, for I know what it means. Nothing looms on the horizon but the hardest five weeks' grind in the world. The next day the practice begins, and for the first time in five months, a uniform is donned. I usually start my work by limbering up slowly, and on the first day I do not pitch at all. With several other players, I help to form a large circle and the time is spent in throwing the ball at impossible and unreachable points in the anatomy. The man next to you shoots one away up over your head and the next one at your feet and off to the side while he is looking at the third man from you. This is great for limbering up, but the loosening is torture. After about fifteen minutes of that, the winter-logged player goes over on the bench and drops down exhausted. But does he stay there?

Not if McGraw sees him, and he is one of the busiest watchers I have ever met.

"Here, Matty," he will shout, "lead this squad three times around the park and be careful not to cut the corners."

By the time that little formality is finished, a man's tongue is hanging out and he goes to get a drink of water. The spring training is just one darned drink after another and still the player is always thirsty.

After three hours of practice, McGraw may say: "All right, Matty. Go back to the hotel and get a bath and a rub and cut it out for to-day."

Or he may remark: "You're looking heavy this year. Better take another little workout this afternoon."

And so, ends the first day. That night I flex the muscles in my salary wing and wonder to myself if it is going to be *very* sore. I get the answer next day. And what always makes me maddest is that the fans up North imagine that we are having some kind of a picnic in Marlin Springs, Texas. My idea of no setting for a pleasure party is Marlin Springs, Texas.

Photo by L. Van Oeyen, Cleveland, Ohio
*Close Play at the Plate*

This picture illustrates how easily the base runner, with his deceptive slide, can get away from the catcher, who has the ball waiting for him. It is always a hard decision for the umpire. Shown in the picture are, left to right, Conroy of Washington, Umpire Evans, and Catcher Land of Cleveland.

The morning of the second day is always a pleasant occasion. The muscles which have remained idle so long begin to rebel at the unaccustomed exercise, and the players are as pleasant as a flock of full-grown grizzly bears. I would not be a waiter for a ball club on a spring tour if they offered me a contract with a salary as large as J. P. Morgan's income.

Each year the winter kinks seem to have settled into the muscles more permanently and are harder to iron out. Of course, there comes a last time for each one of us to go South, and every season I think, on the morning of the second day, when I try to work my muscles, that this one is my last.

The bushers lend variety to the life in a spring camp. Many of them try hard to "horn in" with the men who have made good as Big-Leaguers. When a young player really seems to want to know something, any of the older men will gladly help him, but the trouble with most of them is that they think they are wonders when they arrive.

"How do you hold a curve?" a young fellow asked me last spring.

I showed him.

"Do you think Hans Wagner is as good as Ty Cobb?" he asked me next.

"Listen!" I answered. "Did you come down here to learn to play ball or with the idea that you are attending some sort of a conversational soiree?"

Many recruits think that, if they can get friendly with the veterans, they will be retained on account of their social standing, and I cannot "go" young ballplayers who attempt to become the bootblacks for the old ones. I have seen many a youngster ruin himself, even for playing in the minors, through his too vigorous efforts to make good under the large tent. He will come into camp, and the first day out put everything he has on the ball to show the manager "he's got something."

The Giants had a young pitcher with them in 1911, named Nagle, who tried to pick up the pace, on the first day in camp, at which he had left off on the closing day of the previous year. He started to shoot the ball over to the batters with big, sharp breaking curves on it. He had not been South three days before he developed a sore arm that required a sling to help him carry it around, and he never was able to twirl again before he was shunted back into the lesser leagues.

But hope springs eternal in the breast of the bush leaguer in the spring, and many a young fellow, when he gets his send-off from the little, old hometown, with the local band playing at the station, knows that the next time the populace of that place hears of him, it will be through seeing his name in the headlines of the New York papers. And then along about the middle of April, he comes sneaking back into the old burg, crestfallen and disappointed. There are a lot of humor and some pathos in a spring training trip. Many a busher I have seen go back who has tried hard to make good and just could not, and I have felt sorry for him. It is just like a man in any other business getting a chance at a better job than the one he is holding and not being big enough to fit it. It is the one time that opportunity has knocked, and most of the bush leaguers do not know the combination to open the door, and, as has been pointed out, opportunity was never charged with picking locks. Many are called in the spring, but few get past.

Most of them are sincere young fellows, too, trying to make good, and I have seen them work until their tongues were hanging out and the perspiration was starting all over them, only to hear McGraw say: "I'm sorry, but you will have to go back again. I've let you out to Kankakee."

"Steve Evans", who now plays right field on the St. Louis club, was South with the Giants one season and worked hard to stick. But McGraw had a lot of young out-fielders, and some minor league magnate from Montreal came into camp one day who liked "Steve's" action. McGraw started for the outfield where Evans was chasing flies and tried to get to "Steve," but every time the manager approached him with the minor league man, Evans would rush for a ball on another corner of the field, and he became suddenly hard of hearing.

Steve Evans, St. Louis Cardinals

Finally, McGraw abandoned the chase and let another out-fielder go to Montreal, retaining Evans.

"Say, 'Steve,'" said "Mac," that night, "why didn't you come, when I called you out on the field there this afternoon?"

"Because I could hear the rattle of the tin can you wanted to tie to me, all over the lot," replied Evans.

And eventually, by that subtle dodging, he landed in the Big-League under Bresnahan and has made good out there.

I believe that a pitcher by profession has the hardest time of any of the specialists who go into a spring camp. His work is of a more routine nature than that which attaches to any of the other branches of the baseball art. It is nothing but a steady grind.

The pitcher goes out each morning and gets a catcher with a big mitt and a loud voice and, with a couple of his fellow artists, starts to warm up with this slave-driver.

The right sort of a catcher for spring rehearsing is never satisfied with anything you do. I never try to throw a curve for ten days at least after I get South, for a misplaced curve early in the season may give a man a sore arm for the greater part of the summer, and Big-League clubs are not paying pitchers for wearing crippled whips.

After warming up for an hour or so, three or four pitchers throw slow ones to a batter and try to get the ball on the half bounce and compete as to the number of fumbles. This is great for limbering up.

Then comes the only real enjoyment of the day. It is quick in passing, like a piece of great scenery viewed out of the window of a railroad coach going sixty miles an hour. Each afternoon the regulars play the Yannigans (the spring name of the second team) a game of six innings, and each pitcher has a chance to work about one inning. The batters are away off form and are missing the old round- house curve by two feet that they would hit out of the lot in mid-season. This makes you think for a few minutes that you are a good pitcher. But there is even a drawback to this brief bit of enjoyment, for the diamond at Marlin is skinned—that is, made of dirt, although it is billed as a grass infield, and the ball gets "wingy." Little pieces of the cover are torn loose by contact with the rough dirt, and it is not at all like the hard, smooth, grass-stained ball that is prevalent around the circuit in mid-season. Grass seed has been planted on this infield, but so far, like a lot of bushers, it has failed to make good its promises.

After that game comes the inevitable run around the park which has been a headliner in spring training ever since the institution was discovered.

A story is told of "Cap" Anson and his famous old White Stockings. According to the reports I have heard, training with the "Cap" when he was right was no bed of roses. After hours of practice, he would lead the men in long runs, and the better he felt, the longer the runs.

One hot day, so the story goes, Anson was toiling around the park, with his usual determination, at the head of a string of steaming, sweating players, when "Bill"

"Cap" Anson, Chicago White Stockings

Dahlen, a clever man at finding an opening, discovered a loose board in the fence on the back stretch, pulled it off, and dived through the hole. On the next lap two more tired athletes followed him, and at last the whole squad was on the other side of the fence, watching their leader run on tirelessly. But "Cap" must have missed the "plunk, plunk" of the footsteps behind him, for he looked around and saw that his players were gone. He kept grimly on, alone, until he had finished, and then he pushed his red face through the hole in the fence and saw his men.

"Your turn now, boys," he said, and while he sat in the grand-stand as the sole spectator, he made that crowd of unfortunate athletes run around the track twice as many times as he himself had done.

"Guess I won't have to nail up that hole in the fence, boys," "Cap" remarked when it was all over.

Speaking of the influence of catchers on pitchers during the training trip, there is the well-known case of Wilbert Robinson, the old catcher, and "Rube" Marquard, the great left-handed pitcher of the Giants. "Robbie" devoted himself almost entirely in the spring of 1911 to the training of the then erratic "Rube," and he handed

Wilbert Robinson, New York Giants

back to McGraw at the end of the rehearsal the man who turned out to be the premier pitcher of his League, according to the official figures, and figures are not in the habit of lying.

"Robbie" used to take Marquard off into some corner every day and talk to him for hours. Draw up close, for I am going to tell you the secret of how Marquard became a great pitcher and that, too, at just about the time the papers were mentioning him as the "$11,000 lemon," and imploring McGraw to let him go to some club in exchange for a good capable bat boy.

"Now 'Rube,'" would be "Robbie's" first line in the daily lecture, "you've got to start on the first ball to get the batter. Always have something on him and never let him have anything on you. This is the prescription for a great pitcher."

One of the worst habits of Marquard's early days was to get a couple of strikes on a batter and then let up until he got himself "into a hole" and could not put the ball over. Robinson by his coaching gave him the confidence he lacked.

"'Rube,' you've got a lot of stuff to-day," "Robbie" would advise, "but don't try to get it all on the ball. Mix it with a little control, and it will make a great blend. Now, this guy is a high ball hitter. Let's see you keep it low for him. He waits, so you will have to get it over."

And out there in the hot Texas sun, with much advice and lots of patience, Wilbert Robinson was manufacturing a great pitcher out of the raw material. One of Marquard's worst faults, when he first broke into the League, was that he did not know the batters and their grooves, and these weaknesses Robinson drilled into his head—not that a drill was required to insert the information. Robinson was the coacher, umpire, catcher and batter rolled into one, and as a result look at the "Rube."

When Marquard began to wabble a little toward the end of 1911 and to show some of his old shyness while the club was on its last trip West, Robinson hurried on to Chicago and worked with him for two days. The "Rube" had lost the first game of the series to the Cubs, but he turned around after Robinson joined us and beat them to death in the last contest.

Pitchers, old and young, are always trying for new curves in the spring practice, and out of the South, wafted over the wires by the fertile imaginations of the flotilla of correspondents, drift tales each spring of the "fish" ball and the new "hook" jump and the "stop" ball and many more eccentric curves which usually boil down to modifications of the old ones. I worked for two weeks once on a new, slow, spit ball that would wabble, but the trouble was that I could never tell just when or where it was going to wabble, and so at last I had to abandon it because I could not control it.

After sending out fake stories of new and wonderful curves for several years, at last the correspondents got a new one when the spit ball was first discovered by Stricklett, a Brooklyn pitcher, several seasons ago.

One Chicago correspondent sent back to his paper a glowing tale of the wonderful new curve called the "spit ball," which was obtained by the use of saliva, only to get a wire from his office which read: "It's all right to 'fake' about new curves, but when it comes to being vulgar about it, that's going too far. Either drop that spit ball or mail us your resignation."

The paper refused to print the story and a real new curve was born without its notice. As a matter of fact, Bowerman, the old Giant catcher, was throwing the spit ball for two or three years before it was discovered to be a pitching asset. He used to wet his fingers when catching, and as he threw to second base the ball would take all sorts of eccentric breaks which fooled the baseman, and none could explain why it did it until Stricklett came through with the spit ball.

Elmer Stricklett, Brooklyn Superbas

Many good pitchers, who feel their arms begin to weaken, work on certain freak motions or forms of delivery to make themselves more effective or draw out their baseball life in the Big-Leagues for a year or two. A story is told of "Matty" Kilroy, a left-hander, who lived for two years through the development of what he called the "Bazzazaz" balk, and it had the same effect on his pitching as administering oxygen often has on a patient who is almost dead.

"My old soup bone," says Kilroy, "was so weak that I couldn't break a pane of glass at fifty feet. So, one winter I spent some time every day out in the back yard getting that balk motion down. I had a pretty fair balk motion when my arm was good, but I saw that it had to be better, so I put one stone in the yard for a home plate and another up against the fence for first base. Then I practiced looking at the home plate stone and throwing at first base with a snap of the wrist and without moving my feet. It was stare steady at the batter, then the arm up to about my ear, and zip, with a twist of the wrist at first base, and you've got him!

"Matty" Kilroy, Baltimore Orioles AA

I got so I could throw 'em harder to the bag with that wrist wriggle than I could to the batter and I had them stickin' closer to the base for two years than a sixteen-year-old fellow does to his gal when they've just decided they would do for each other."

As a rule, McGraw takes charge of the batters and general teamwork at spring practice, and he is one of the busiest little persons in seven counties, for he says a lot depends on the start a club gets in a league race. He always wants the first jump because it is lots easier falling back than catching up.

After a week or so of practice, the team is divided up into two squads, and one goes to San Antonio and the other to Houston each Saturday and Sunday to play games. One of the older men takes charge of the younger players, and there is a lot of rivalry between the two teams to see which one will make the better record, I remember one year I was handling the youngsters, and we went to Houston to play the team there and just managed to nose out a victory. McGraw thought that for the next Saturday he had better strengthen the Yannigans up a bit, so he sent Roger Bresnahan along to play third base instead of Henderson, the young fellow we had the week before. Playing third base could not exactly have been called a habit with "Rog" at that time. He was still pretty fat, and bending over quick after grounders was not his regular line. He booted two or three and finally managed to lose the game for us.

We sent McGraw the following telegram that night: "John McGraw, manager of the Giants, San Antonio, Texas: "Will trade Bresnahan for Henderson. Rush answer."

McGraw does not like to have any of his clubs beaten by

the minor leaguers, because the bushers are inclined to imitate pouter pigeons right away after beating the Big-Leaguers.

The social side of a training trip consists of kicking about the grub, singing songs at night, and listening to the same old stories that creep out of the bushes on crutches year after year. Last spring the food got so bad that some of the newspaper men fixed up a fake story they said they were going to send to New York, displayed it to the proprietor, and he came through with beefsteak for three nights in succession, thus establishing a record and proving the power of the press. The trouble with the diet schedule on a spring trip is that almost invariably those hotels on the bush-league circuits serve dinner in the middle of the day, just when a ball-player does not feel like eating anything much. Then at night they have a pick-up supper when one's stomach feels as if it thought a fellow's throat had been cut.

The Giants had an umpire with them in the spring of 1911, named Hansell, who enlivened the long, weary, training season some. Like a lot of the recruits who thought that they were great ballplayers, this Hansell firmly believed he was a great umpire. He used to try to put players who did not agree with his decisions out of the game and, of course, they would not go.

"Why don't you have them arrested if they won't leave?" McGraw asked him one day. "I would."

So, the next afternoon Hansell had a couple of the local constables out at the grounds and tried to have Devore pinched for kicking on a decision. "Josh" got sore and framed it up to have a camera man at the park the next day to take a moving picture of a mob scene, Hansell, the umpire, to be the hero and mobbed. Hansell fell for it until he saw all the boys picking up real clods and digging the dirt out of their spikes, and then he made a run for it and never came back. That is how we lost a great umpire.

"You boys made it look too realistic for him," declared McGraw.

Hansell had a notion that he was a runner and offered to bet Robinson, who is rather corpulent now, that he could beat him running across the field. Robinson took him and walked home ahead of the umpire in the race.

"I don't see where I get off on this deal," complained McGraw when it was over. "I framed up this race for you two fellows, and then Hansell comes to me and borrows the ten to pay 'Robbie.'"

Somebody fixed up a Turkish bath in the hotel one day by stuffing up the cracks in one of the bathrooms and turning the hot water into the tub and the steam into the radiator full blast.

Several towels were piled on the radiator and the players sat upon this swathed in blankets to take off weight. They entered the impromptu Turkish bath, wearing only the well-known smile. McGraw still maintains that it was "Bugs" Raymond who pulled out the towels when it came the manager's turn to sit on the radiator, and, if he could have proved his case, Raymond would not have needed a doctor. It would have been time for the undertaker.

Finally comes the long wending of the way up North. "Bugs" Raymond always depends on his friends for his refreshments, and as he had few friends in Marlin in 1911, he got few drinks. But when we got to Dallas cocktails were served with the dinner and all the ballplayers left them untouched, McGraw enforcing the old rule that lips that touch "licker" shall never moisten a spit ball for him. "Bugs" was missed after supper and someone found him out in the kitchen licking up all the discarded Martinis.

That was the occasion of his first fine of the season, and after that, as "Bugs" himself admitted, "life for him was just one fine after another."

At last, after the long junket through the South, on which all managers are Simon Legrees, is ended, comes a welcome day, when the new uniforms are donned and the band plays and "them woids" which constitute the sweetest music to the ears of a ball-player, roll off the tongue of the umpire: "The batteries for to-day are

Rucker and Bergen for Brooklyn, Marquard and Meyers for New York. Play ball!" The season is on.

"Nap" Rucker, Brooklyn Dodgers

# Jinxes and What They Mean to a Ball-Player

*A Load of Empty Barrels, Hired by John McGraw, once Pulled the Giants out of a Losing Streak—The Child of Superstition Appears to the Ball-Player in Many Forms—Various Ways in which the Influence of the Jinx can be Overcome—The True Story of "Charley" Faust—The Necktie that Helped Win a Pennant.*

**A FRIEND** of mine, who took a different fork in the road when we left college from the one that I have followed, was walking down Broadway in New York with me one morning after I had joined the Giants, and we passed a cross-eyed man. I grabbed off my hat and spat in it. It was a new hat, too. "What's the matter with you, Matty?" he asked, surprised.

"Spit in your hat quick and kill that jinx," I answered, not thinking for the minute, and he followed my example.

I forgot to mention, when I said he took another fork in the road, that he had become a pitcher, too, but of a different kind. He had turned out to be sort of a conversational pitcher, for he was a minister, and, as luck would have it, on the morning we met that cross-eyed man he was wearing a silk hat. I was shocked, pained, and mortified when I saw what I had made him do. But he was the right sort and wanted to go through with the thing according to the standards of the professional man with whom he happened to be at the time.

"What's the idea?" he asked as he replaced his hat.

"Worst jinx in the world to see a cross-eyed man," I replied. "But I hope I didn't hurt your silk hat," I quickly apologized.

"Not at all. But how about these ballplayers who masticate the weed? Do they kill jinxes, too?" he wanted to know.

And I had to admit that they were the main exterminators of the jinx. "Then," he went on, "I'm glad that the percentage of wearers of cross eyes is small."

I have just looked into one of my favorite works for that word "jinx," and found it not. My search was in Webster's dictionary. But any ballplayer can give a definition of it with his hands tied behind him—that is, anyone except "Arlie" Latham, and, with his hands bound, he is deaf and dumb.

A jinx is something which brings bad luck to a ball-player, and the members of the profession have built up a series of lucky and unlucky omens that should be catalogued. And besides the common or garden variety of jinxes, many stars have a series of private or pet and trained ones that are more malignant in their forms than those which come out in the open.

A jinx is the child of superstition, and ballplayers are among the most superstitious persons in the world, notwithstanding all this conversation lately about educated men breaking into the game and paying no attention whatever to the good and bad omens. College men are coming into both the leagues, more of them each year, and they are doing their share to make the game better and the class of men higher, but they fall the hardest for the jinxes. And I don't know as it is anything to be ashamed of at that.

A really true, on-the-level, honest-to-jiminy jinx can do all sorts of mean things to a professional ballplayer. I have seen it make a bad pitcher out of a good one, and a blind batter out of a three- hundred hitter, and I have seen it make a ball club, composed of educated men, carry a Kansas farmer, with two or three screws rattling loose in his dome, around the circuit because he came as a prophet and said that he was accompanied by Miss Fickle Fortune. And that is almost a jinx record.

Jinx and Miss Fickle Fortune never go around together. And ballplayers are always trying to kill this jinx, for, once he joins the club, all hope is gone. He dies hard, and many a good hat has been ruined in an effort to destroy him, as I have said before, because the wearer happened to be chewing tobacco when the jinx dropped around. But what's a new hat against a losing streak or a batting slump?

Luck is a combination of confidence and getting the breaks. Ballplayers get no breaks without confidence in themselves, and lucky omens inspire this confidence. On the other hand, unlucky signs take it away. The lucky man is the one who hits the nail on the head and not his fingers, and the ability to swat the nail on its receptive end is a combination of self-confidence and an aptitude for hammering. Good ball-playing is the combination of self-confidence and the ability to play.

The next is "Red" Ames, although designated as "Leon" by his family when a very small boy before he began to play ball. (He is still called "Leon" in the winter.) Ames is of Warren, Ohio, and the Giants, and he is said to hold the Marathon record for being the most unlucky pitcher that ever lived, and I agree with the sayers.

Leon "Red" Ames, New York Giants

For several seasons, Ames couldn't seem to win a ball game, no matter how well he pitched. In 1909, "Red" twirled a game on the opening day of the season against Brooklyn that was the work of a master. For nine innings he held his opponents hitless, only to have them win in the thirteenth. Time and again Ames has pitched brilliantly, to be finally beaten by a small score, because one of the men behind him made an error at a critical moment, or because the team could not give him any runs by which to win. No wonder the newspapers began to speak of Ames as the "hoodoo" pitcher and the man "who couldn't win."

There was a cross-eyed fellow who lived between Ames and the Polo Grounds, and "Red" used to make a detour of several blocks en route to the park to be sure to miss him in case he should be out walking. But one day in 1911, when it was his turn to pitch, he bumped into that cross-eyed man and, in spite of the fact that he did his duty by his hat and got three or four small boys to help him out, he failed to last two innings. When it came time to go West on the final trip of the 1911 season, Ames was badly discouraged.

"I don't see any use in taking me along, Mac," he said to McGraw a few days before we left.

"The club can't win with me pitching if the other guys don't even get a foul."

The first stop was in Boston, and on the day we arrived it rained. In the mail that day, addressed to Leon Ames, came a necktie and a four-leaf clover from a prominent actress, wishing Ames good luck. The directions were inside the envelope. The four-leaf clover, if the charm were to work, must be worn on both the uniform and street clothes, and the necktie was to be worn with the street clothes and concealed in the uniform, if that necktie could be concealed anywhere. It would have done for a headlight and made Joseph's coat of many colors look like a mourning garment.

"Might as well wish good luck to a guy on the way to the morgue," murmured Ames as he surveyed the layout, but he manfully put on the necktie, taking his first dose of the prescription, as directed, at once, and he tucked the four-leaf clover away carefully in his wallet.

"You've got your work cut out for you, old boy," he remarked to the charm as he put it away, "but I'd wear you if you were a horseshoe."

The first day that Ames pitched in Boston he won and won in a stroll.

"The necktie," he explained that night at dinner, and pointed to the three-sheet, colored-supplement affair he was wearing around his collar, "I don't change her until I lose."

*And he didn't lose a game on that trip.* Once he almost did, when he was taken out in the sixth inning, and a batter put in for him, but the Giants finally pulled out the victory and he got the credit for it. He swept through the West unbeatable, letting down Pittsburg with two or three hits, cleaning up in St. Louis, and finally breaking our losing streak in Chicago after two games had gone against us. And all the time he wore that spectrum around his collar for a necktie. As it frayed with the wear and tear, more colors began to show, although I didn't think it possible. If he had had occasion to put on his evening clothes, I believe that tie would have gone with it.

For my part, I would almost rather have lost a game and changed the necktie, since it gave one the feeling all the time that he was carrying it around with him because he had had the wrong end of an election bet, or something of the sort. But not Ames! He was a game guy. He stuck with the necktie, and it stuck with him, and the combination kept right on winning ball games. Maybe he didn't mind it because he could not see it himself, unless he looked in a mirror, but it was rough on the rest of the team, except that we needed the games the necktie won, to take the pennant.

Columns were printed in the newspapers about that necktie, and it became the most famous scarf in the world. Ames used to sleep with it under his pillow alongside of his bank roll, and he didn't lose another game until the very end of the season, when he dropped one against Brooklyn.

"I don't hardly lay that up against the tie," he said afterwards. "You see, Mac put all those youngsters into it, and I didn't get any support."

Analyzing is a distasteful pastime to me, but let's see what it was that made Ames win. Was it the necktie? Perhaps not. But some sliver of confidence, which resulted from that first game when he was dressed up in the scarf and the four-leaf clover, got stuck in his mind. And after that the rest was easy.

Frank Chance, the manager of the Cubs, has a funny superstition which is of the personal sort. Most ballplayers have a natural prejudice against the number "13" in any form, but particularly when attached to a

Pullman berth. But Chance always insists, whenever possible, that he have "lower 13." He says that if he can just crawl in under that number, he is sure of a good night's rest, a safe journey, and a victory the next day. He has been in two or three minor railroad accidents, and he declares that all these occurred when he was sleeping on some other shelf besides "lower 13." He can usually satisfy his hobby, too, for most travelers steer clear of the berth.

McGraw believes a stateroom brings him good luck, or at least he always insists on having one when he can get it. "Chance can have 'lower 13,'" says "Mac," "but give me a stateroom for luck."

Most ballplayers nowadays treat the superstitions of the game as jokes, probably because they are a little ashamed to acknowledge their weaknesses, but away down underneath they observe the proprieties of the ritual. Why, even I won't warm up with the third baseman while I am waiting for the catcher to get on his mask and the rest of his paraphernalia. Once, when I first broke in with the Giants, I warmed up with the third baseman between innings and in the next round they hit me hard and knocked me out of the box. Since then, I have had an uncommon prejudice against the practice, and I hate to hear a man even mention it.

Devlin knows of my weakness and never suggests it when he is playing the bag, but occasionally a new performer will drill into the box score at third base and yell: "Come on, Matty! Warm up here while you're waiting."

It gets me. I'll pitch to the first baseman or a substitute catcher to keep warm, but I would rather freeze to death than heat up with the third baseman. That is one of my pet jinxes.

And speaking of Arthur Devlin, he has a few hand-raised jinxes of his own, too. For instance, he never likes to hear a player hum a tune on the bench, because he thinks it will keep him from getting a base hit. He nearly beat a youngster to death one day when he kept on humming after Devlin had told him to stop.

"Cut that out, Caruso," yelled Arthur, as the recruit started his melody. "You are killing base hits."

The busher continued with his air until Devlin tried another form of persuasion.

Arthur also has a favorite seat on the bench which he believes is luckier than the rest, and he insists on sitting in just that one place.

But the worst blow Devlin ever had was when some young lady admirer of his in his palmy days, who unfortunately wore her eyes crossed, insisted on sitting behind third base for each game, so as to be near him.

Arthur noticed her one day and, after that, it was all off. He hit the worst slump of his career. For a while no one could understand it, but at last he confessed to McGraw. "Mac," he said one night in the club-house, "it's that jinx. Have you noticed her? She sits behind the bag every day, and she has got me going. She has sure slid the casters under me. I wish we could bar her out, or poison her, or shoot her, or chloroform her, or kill her in some nice, mild way because, if it isn't done, this League is going to lose a ball-player. How can you expect a guy to play with that overlooking him every afternoon?"

McGraw took Devlin out of the game for a time after that, and the newspapers printed several yards about the cross-eyed jinx who had ruined the Giants' third baseman.

With the infield weakened by the loss of Devlin, the club began to lose with great regularity. But one day the jinxess was missing and she never came back. She must have read in the newspapers what she was doing to Devlin, her hero, and quit the national pastime or moved to another part of the stand. With this weight off his shoulders, Arthur went back into the game and played like mad.

"If she'd stuck much longer," declared McGraw, joyous in his rejuvenated third baseman, "I would have had her eyes operated on and straightened. This club couldn't afford to keep on losing ball games because you are such a Romeo, Arthur, that even the cross-eyed ones fall for you."

Ballplayers are very superstitious about the bats. Did you ever notice how the clubs are all laid out in a neat, even row before the bench and are scrupulously kept that way by the bat boy?

If one of the sticks by any chance gets crossed, all the players will shout: "Uncross the bats! Uncross the bats!"

It's as bad as discovering a three-alarm fire in an excelsior factory. Don't believe it? Then listen to what happened to the Giants once because a careless bat boy neglected his duty. The team was playing in Cincinnati in the season of 1906 when one of the bats got crossed through the carelessness of the boy. What was the result? "Mike" Donlin, the star slugger of the team, slid into third base and came up with a broken ankle.

Ever since that time we have carried our own boy with us, because a club with championship aspirations cannot afford to take a chance with those foreign artists handling the bats. They are likely to throw you down at any time.

The Athletics have a funny superstition which is private or confined to their team as far as I know. When luck seems to be breaking against them in a game, they will take the bats and throw them wildly into the air and let them lie around in front of their bench, topsy-turvy. They call this changing the luck, but any other club would consider that it was the worst kind of a jinx. It is the same theory that card-players have about shuffling the deck vigorously to bring a different run of fortune. Then, if the luck changes, the Athletics throw the bats around some more to keep it. This act nearly cost them one of their best ballplayers in the third game of the 1911 world's series.

The Philadelphia players had tossed their bats to break their run of luck, for the score was 1 to 0 against them, when Baker came up in the ninth inning. He cracked his now famous home run into the right-field bleachers, and the men on the bench hurled the bats wildly into the air. In jumping up and reaching for a bat to throw, Jack Barry, the shortstop, hit his head on the concrete roof of the structure and was stunned for a minute. He said that little black specks were floating in front of his eyes, but he gamely insisted on playing the contest out. "Connie" Mack was so worried over his condition that he sent Ira Thomas out on the field to inquire if he were all right, and this interrupted the game in the ninth inning. A lot of the spectators thought that Thomas was out there, bearing some secret message from "Connie" Mack. None knew that he was ascertaining the health of a player who had almost killed himself while killing a jinx.

The Athletics, for two seasons, have carried with them on all their trips a combination bat boy and mascot who is a hunchback, and he outjinxed our champion jinx killer, Charley Faust, in the 1911 world's series. A hunchback is regarded by ballplayers as the best luck in the world. If a man can just touch that hump on the way to the plate, he is sure to get a hit, and any observant spectator will notice the Athletics' hitters rubbing the hunchback boy before leaving the bench. So attached to this boy have the players become that they voted him half a share of the prize money last year after the world's series. Lots of ballplayers would tell you that he deserved it because he has won two world's pennants for them.

Another great piece of luck is for a ball-player to rub a colored kid's head. I've walked along the street with ballplayers and seen them stop a young negro and take off his hat and run their hands through his kinky hair. Then I've seen the same ball-player go out and get two or three hits that afternoon and play the game of his life. Again, it is the confidence inspired, coupled with the ability.

Another old superstition among ballplayers is that a load of empty barrels means base hits. If an athlete can just pass a flock of them on the way to the park, he is sure to step right along stride for stride with the three-hundred hitters that afternoon.

McGraw once broke up a batting slump of the Giants with a load of empty barrels. That is why I maintain he is the greatest manager of them all. He takes advantage of the little things, even the superstitions of his men, and turns them to his account. He played this trick in one of the first years that he managed the New York club. The batting of all the players had slumped at the same time. None could hit, and the club was losing game after game as a result, because the easiest pitchers were making the best batters look foolish.

One day Bowerman came into the clubhouse with a smile on his face for the first time in a week. "Saw a big load of empty barrels this afternoon, boys," he announced, "and just watch me pickle the pill out there today."

Frank Bowerman, New York Giants

Right at that point McGraw got an idea, as he frequently does. Bowerman went out that afternoon and made four hits out of a possible five. The next day three or four more of the players came into the park, carrying smiles and the announcement that fortunately they, too, had met a load of empty barrels.

They, then, all went out and regained their old batting strides, and we won that afternoon for the first time in a week. More saw a load of barrels the next day and started to bat. At last, all the members of the team had met the barrels, and men with averages of .119 were threatening to chisel into the three-hundred set. With remarkable regularity the players were meeting loads of empty barrels on their way to the park, and, with remarkable regularity and a great deal of expedition, the pitchers of opposing clubs were being driven to the shower bath.

"Say," asked "Billy" Gilbert, the old second baseman of "Bill" Lauder, formerly the protector of the third corner, one day, "is one of that team of horses sorrel and the other white?"

"Sure," answered "Bill."

"Sure," echoed McGraw. "I hired that load of empty barrels by the week to drive around and meet you fellows on the way to the park, and you don't think I can afford to have them change horses every day, do you?"

"Billy" Gilbert, New York Giants

Everybody had a good laugh and kept on swatting. McGraw asked for waivers on the load of empty barrels soon afterwards, but his scheme had stopped a batting slump and put the club's hitters on their feet again. He plays to the little personal qualities and

"Bill" Lauder, New York Giants

superstitions in the men to get the most out of them. And just seeing those barrels gave them the idea that they were bound to get the base hits, and they got them. Once more, the old confidence, hitched up with ability.

What manager would have carried a Kansas farmer around the circuit with him besides McGraw?

I refer to Charles Victor Faust of Marion, Kansas, the most famous jinx killer of them all. Faust first met the Giants in St. Louis on the next to the last trip the club made West in the season of 1911, when he wandered into the Planter's Hotel one day, asked for McGraw and announced that a fortune teller of Marion had informed him he would be a great pitcher and that for $5 he could have a full reading.

This pitching announcement piqued Charles, and he reached down into his jeans, dug out his last five, and passed it over. The fortune teller informed Faust that all he had to do to get into the headlines of the newspapers and to be a great pitcher was to join the New York Giants. He joined, and, after he once joined, it would have taken the McNamaras in their best form to separate him from the said Giants.

"Charley" came out to the ballpark and amused himself warming up. Incidentally, the Giants did not lose a game while he was in the neighborhood. The night the club left for Chicago on that trip, he was down at the Union Station ready to go along.

"Did you get your contract and transportation?" asked McGraw, as the lanky Kansan appeared.

"No," answered "Charley."

"Pshaw," replied McGraw. "I left it for you with the clerk at the hotel. The train leaves in two minutes," he continued, glancing at his watch. "If you can run the way you say you can, you can make it and be back in time to catch it."

It was the last we saw of "Charley" Faust for a time—galloping up the platform in his angular way with that contract and transportation in sight.

"I'm almost sorry we left him," remarked McGraw as "Charley" disappeared in the crowd.

"Charley" Faust, New York Giants

We played on around the circuit with indifferent luck and got back to New York with the pennant no more than a possibility, and rather a remote one at that.

The first day we were in New York "Charley" Faust entered the clubhouse with several inches of dust and mud caked on him, for he had come all the way either by side-door special or blind baggage. "I'm here, all right," he announced quietly, and started to climb into a uniform.

239

"I see you are," answered McGraw.

"Charley" stuck around for two or three days, and we won. Then McGraw decided he would have to be dropped and ordered the man on the door of the clubhouse to bar this Kansas kid out. Faust broke down and cried that day, and we lost. After that he became a member of the club, and we won game after game until some busy newspaper man obtained a vaudeville engagement for him at a salary of $100 a week.

We lost three games the week he was absent from the grounds, and Faust saw at once he was not doing the right thing by the club, so, with a wave of his hand that would have gone with J. P. Morgan's income, he passed up some lucrative vaudeville contracts, much to the disgust of the newspaper man, who was cutting the remuneration with him, and settled down to business.

The club did not lose a game after that, and it was decided to take Faust West with us on the last and famous trip in 1911. Daily he had been bothering McGraw and Mr. Brush for his contract, for he wanted to pitch. The club paid him some money from time to time to meet his personal expenses.

The Sunday night the club left for Boston, a vaudeville agent was at the Grand Central Station with a contract offering Faust $100 a week for five weeks, which "Charley" refused in order to stick with the club. It was the greatest trip away from home in the history of baseball. Starting with the pennant almost out of reach, the Giants won eighteen and lost four games. One contest that we dropped in St. Louis was when some of the newspaper correspondents on the trip kidnapped Faust and sat him on the St. Louis bench.

Another day in St. Louis the game had gone eleven innings, and the Cardinals needed one run to win. They had several incipient scores on the bases and "Rube" Marquard, in the box, was apparently going up in the air. Only one was out. Faust was warming up far in the suburbs when, under orders from McGraw, I ran out and sent him to the bench, for that was the place from which his charm seemed to be the most potent. "Charley" came loping to the bench as fast as his long legs would transport him and St. Louis didn't score and we won the game. It was as nice a piece of pinch 'mascoting' as I ever saw.

The first two games that "Charley" really lost were in Chicago. And all through the trip, he reiterated his weird prophecies that "the Giants with Manager McGraw were goin' ta win." The players believed in him, and none would have let him go if it had been necessary to support him out of their own pockets.

And we did win.

"Charley," with his monologue and great good humor, kept the players in high spirits throughout the journey, and the feeling prevailed that we couldn't lose with him along. He was advertised all over the circuit, and spectators were going to the ballpark to see Faust and

Wagner. "Charley" admitted that he could fan out Hans because he had learned how to pitch out there in Kansas by correspondence school and had read of "Hans's" weakness in a book. His one "groove" was massages and manicures. He would go into the barber shop with any member of the team who happened to be getting shaved and take a massage and manicure for the purposes of sociability, as a man takes a drink. He easily was the record holder for the manicure Marathon, hanging up the figures of five in one day in St. Louis. He also liked pie for breakfast, dinner and supper, and a small half before retiring.

But alas! "Charley" lost in the world's series. He couldn't make good. And a jinx killer never comes back. He is gone. And his expansive smile and bump-the-bumps slide are gone with him. That is, McGraw hopes he is gone. But he was a wonder while he had it. And he did a great deal toward giving the players confidence. With him on the bench, they thought they couldn't lose, and they couldn't. It has long been a superstition among ballplayers that when a "bug" joins a club, it will win a championship, and the Giants believed it when "Charley" Faust arrived. Did "Charley" Faust win the championship for the Giants?

Another time-honored superstition among ballplayers is that no one must say to a pitcher as he goes to the box for the eighth inning: "Come on, now. Only six more men."

Or for the ninth: "Pitch hard, now. Only three left."

Ames says that he lost a game in St. Louis once because McGraw forgot himself and urged him to pitch hard because only three remained to be put out.

Those three batters raised the mischief with Ames's prospects; he was knocked out of the box in that last inning, and we lost the game. That was before the days of the wonder necktie.

Ames won the third game played in Chicago on the last trip West. Coming into the ninth inning, he had the Cubs beaten, when McGraw began: "Come on, 'Red,' only——"

"Nix, Mac," cut in Ames, "for the love of Mike, be reasonable."

And then he won the game. But the chances are that if McGraw had got that "only three more" out, he would have lost, because it would have been working on his strained nerves.

# Base Runners and How They Help a Pitcher to Win

*The Secret of Successful Base Running is Getting the Start—A Club Composed of Good Base Runners Is Likely to do More to Help a Pitcher Win Games than a Batting Order of Hard Hitters—Stealing Second Is an Art in Taking Chances—The Giants Stole their Way to a Pennant, but "Connie" Mack Stopped the Grand Larceny when it Came to a World's Championship.*

**MANY TIMES,** have the crowds at the Polo Grounds seen a man get on first base in a close game, and, with the pitcher's motion, start to steal second, only to have the catcher throw him out. The spectators groan and criticize the manager.

"Why didn't he wait for the hitters to bat him around?" is the cry.

Then, again, a man starts for the base, times his getaway just right, and slides into the bag in a cloud of dust while the umpire spreads out his hands indicating that he is safe. The crowd cheers and proclaims McGraw a great manager and the stealer a great base runner. Maybe the next batter comes along with a hit, and the runner scores. It wins the game, and mention is made in the newspapers the next morning of the fast base running of the club. A man has covered ninety feet of ground while the ball is travelling from the pitcher to the catcher and back to the fielder who is guarding second base. It is the most important ninety feet in baseball. From second base just one hit scores the runner. Stealing second, one of the most picturesque plays of the game, is the gentle art of taking a chance.

In 1911, the Giants stole more bases than any other Big-League club has had to its credit since the Pirates established the record in 1903. Devore, Snodgrass, Murray, Merkle and Doyle, once they got on the bases were like loose mercury. They couldn't be caught. And McGraw stole his way to a pennant with this quintet of runners, not alone because of the number of bases they pilfered, but because of the edge it gave the Giants on the rest of the clubs, with the men with base-stealing reputations on the team. I should say that holding these runners up on the bases and worrying about what they were going to do reduced the efficiency of opposing pitchers one-third.

It wasn't the speed of the men that accounted for the record. A sprinter may get into the Big-League and never steal a base. But it was the McGraw system combined with their natural ability.

"Get the start," reiterates McGraw. "Half of base stealing is leaving the bag at the right time. Know when you have a good lead and then never stop until you have hit the dirt."

It is up to the pitcher as much as the catcher to stop base stealing, for once a club begins running wild on another, the bats might as well be packed up and the game conceded. Pitchers make a study of the individual runners and their styles of getting starts. In my mind, I know just how much of a lead every base runner in the National League can take on me with impunity.

"Bob" Bescher of the Cincinnati club was the leading, bright, particular base-stealing star of the National League in the season of 1911, and the secret of his success was in his start. He tries to get as big a lead as possible with each pitch, and then, when he intends to leave, edges a couple of feet farther than usual, catching the pitcher unawares. With the two extra feet, Bescher is bound to get to second base at the same time as the ball, and no catcher in the world can stop him.

"Bob" Bescher, Cincinnati Reds

Therefore, it is up to the pitcher to keep him from getting this start—the two more feet he seeks. I know that Bescher can take ten feet from the bag when I am pitching and get back safely. But I am equally sure that, if he makes his lead twelve feet and I notice it, I can probably catch him. As a good ribbon salesman constantly has in his mind's eye the answer to the question, "How far is a yard?" so I know at a glance exactly how far Bescher can lead and get back safely, when he is on first base. If I glance over and see him twelve feet away from the bag and about to start, I turn and throw and catch him flat-footed.

The crowd laughs at him and says: "Bescher asleep at the switch again!"

The real truth is that Bescher was not asleep, but trying to get that old jump which would have meant the stolen base. Again, he takes the twelve feet, and I don't perceive it. He gets started with my arm and goes into the bag ahead of the ball.

"Great base runner," comments the fickle crowd.

Bescher has only accomplished what he was trying to do before, but he has gotten away with it this time. Being a great ball-player is the gentle art of getting away with it. Spectators often wonder why a pitcher wearies them with throwing over to the first base many times, when it is plain to see that he has no chance of catching his quarry. "Bill" Dahlen used to be one of the best men in the game for getting back in some way when on base, employing a straddle slide and just hooking the bag with his toe, leaving "a shoe-string to touch." The result was that he was always handing the pitcher the laugh as he brushed himself off, for none can say Dahlen was not an immaculate ball-player.

But the pitchers found out that they could tire Dahlen out by repeatedly throwing over to the bag, and that, after five throws, which required five dashes and slides back to the base, he was all in and could not steal because he didn't have the physical strength left. Thus, as soon as Dahlen got on, a pitcher began throwing over until he had him tired out, and then he pitched to the batter. So "Bill" crossed them by living on the bag until he thought he saw his opportunity to get the jump, and then he would try to steal.

Few good base runners watch the ball after they have once left the bag. They look at the baseman to see how he is playing and make the slide accordingly. If Devore sees Huggins of St. Louis behind the base, he slides in front and pulls his body away from the bag, so that he leaves the smallest possible area to touch. If he observes the baseman cutting inside to block him off, he goes behind and hooks it with just one toe, again presenting the minimum touching surface. If the ball is hit while the runner is en route, he takes one quick glance at the coacher on the third base line and can tell by his motions whether to turn back or to continue.

Miller Huggins, St. Louis Cardinals

McGraw devotes half his time and energy in the spring to teaching his men base running and the art of sliding, which, when highly cultivated, means being there with one toe and somewhere else with the rest of the body. But most of all he impresses on the athletes the necessity of getting the start before making the attempt to steal. As long as I live I shall believe that if Snodgrass had known he had the jump in the third game of the world's series in 1911, when he really had it, and if he had taken advantage of it, we would have won the game and possibly the championship. It was in the contest that Baker balanced by banging the home run into the right field bleachers in the ninth inning, when I was pitching. That tied the score, 1 to 1.

For nine innings I had been pitching myself out, putting everything that I had on every ball, because the team gave me no lead to rest on. When Baker pushed that ball into the bleachers with only two more men to get out to win the game, I was all in. But I managed to live through the tenth with very little on the ball, and we came to the bat. Snodgrass got a base on balls and journeyed to second on a sacrifice. He was taking a big lead off the middle base with the pitcher's motion, and running back before the catcher got the ball, because a quick throw would have caught him. It was bad baseball, but he was nervous with the intense strain and over-eager to score.

Then came the time when he took a longer lead than any other, and Lapp, the Athletics' catcher, seeing him, was sure he was going to steal, and in his hurry to get the ball away and save the game, let it past him. Snodgrass had the jump, and probably would have made the base had he kept on going, but he had no orders to steal and had turned and taken a step or two back toward second when he saw Lapp lose the ball. Again, he turned and retraced his steps, and I never saw a man turn so slowly, simply because I realized how important a turn that was going to be.

Next, I looked at Lapp and saw him picking up the ball, which had rolled only about three feet behind him. He snapped it to third and had Snodgrass by several feet. Snodgrass realized this as he plunged down the base line, but he could not stop and permit himself to be tagged and he could not go back, so he made that historic slide, which was heard almost around the world, cut off several yards of Frank Baker's trousers, and more important than the damage to the uniform, lost us the game.

Jack Lapp, Philadelphia Athletics

Snodgrass had the jump in his first start, and if he had kept right on going, he would have made the bag without the aid of the passed ball, in my opinion. But he did not know that he had this advantage and was on his way back when it looked for a minute as if the Athletics' catcher had made a mistake. This really turned out to be the "break" in the game, for it was on that passed ball that Snodgrass was put out. He would probably have scored the run which would have won the game had he lived either on second or third base, for a hit followed.

After losing the contest after watching the opportunity thrown away, some fan called me on the telephone that night, when I was feeling in anything but a conversational mood, and asked me: "Was that passed ball this afternoon part of the Athletics' inside game? Did Lapp do it on purpose?"

In passing I want to put in a word for Snodgrass, not because he is a team-mate of mine, but on account of the criticism which he received for spiking Baker, and which was not deserved. And in that word, I do not want to detract from Baker's reputation a scintilla, if I could, for he is a great ball-player. But I want to say that if John Murray had ever been called upon to slide into that bag with Baker playing it as he did, Baker would probably have been found cut in halves, and only Murray's own style of coasting would have been responsible for it. If Fred Clarke of Pittsburg had been the man coming in, Baker would probably have been neatly cut into thirds, one third with each foot.

Clarke is known as one of the most wicked sliders in the National League. He jumps into the air and spreads his feet apart, showing his spikes as he comes in. The Giants were playing in Pittsburg several years ago, before I was married, and there was a friend of mine at the ballpark with whom I was particularly eager to make a hit. The game was close, as are all contests which lend themselves readily to an anecdote, and Clarke got as far as third base in the eighth inning, with the score tied and two out. Warner, the Giants' catcher, let one get past him and I ran in to cover the plate. Clarke came digging for home and, as I turned to touch him, he slid and cut my trousers off, never touching my legs. It was small consolation to me that my stems were still whole and that the umpire had called Clarke out and that the game was yet saved. My love for my art is keen, but it stops at a certain point, and that point is where I have to send a hurry call for a barrel and the team's tailor. The players made a sort of group around me while I did my Lady Godiva act from the plate to the bench.

Murray has the ideal slide for a base gatherer, but one which commands the respect of all the guardians of the sacks in the National League. When about eight feet from the bag, he jumps into the air, giving the fielder a vision of two sets of nicely honed spikes aimed for the base. As Murray hits the bag, he comes up on his feet and is in a position to start for the next station in case of any fumble or slip. He is a great man to use this slide to advantage against young players, who are inclined to be timid when they see those spikes. It's all part of the game as it is played in the large leagues.

The Boston team was trying out a young player two years ago.

Murray remarked to McGraw before the game: "The first time I get on, I bet I can make that fellow fumble and pick up an extra base."

"Theatre tickets for the crowd on Saturday night?" inquired McGraw.

"You've said it," answered Murray.

John "Red" Murray, New York Giants

Along about the second or third inning John walked and started for second on the first ball pitched.

The busher came in to cover the base, and Murray leaped clear of the ground and yelled: "Look out!"

The newcomer evidently thought that Murray had lost control of his legs, got one look at those spikes, and bent all his energies toward dodging them, paying no attention whatever to the ball, which continued its unmolested journey to center field. The new man proved to be one of the best little dodgers I ever saw. John was in a perfect position to start and went along to third at his leisure.

"Didn't I call the turn?" Murray yelled at McGraw as he came to the bench.

"What show do you want to see?" asked McGraw. But on an old campaigner this show of spikes has no effect whatever. The capable basemen in the League know how to cover the bag so as to get the runner out and still give him room to come in without hurting anyone. In spite of an impression that prevails to the contrary, ballplayers never spike a man on purpose. At present, I don't believe there is a runner in the National League who would cut down another man if he had the opportunity. If one man does spike another accidentally, he is heartily sorry, and often such an event affects his own playing and his base running ability.

The feet-first slide is now more in vogue in the Big-Leagues than the old head-first coast, and I attribute this to two causes. One is that the show of the spikes is a sort of assurance the base runner is going to have room to come into the bag, and the second is that the great amount of armor which a catcher wears in these latter days makes some such formidable slide necessary when coming into the plate.

If a base runner hits a catcher squarely with his shin guards on, he is likely to be badly injured, and he must be sure that the catcher is going to give him a clear path. Some catchers block off the plate so that a man has got to shoot his spikes at them to get through, and I'm not saying that it's bad catching, because that is the way to keep a man from scoring. Make him go around if possible.

But the game has changed in the last few years as far as intentional spiking goes. Many a time, when I first started with the Giants, I heard a base runner shout at a fielder: "Get out of the way there or I'll cut you in two!"

And he would not have hesitated to do it, either. That was part of the game. But nowadays, if a player got the reputation of cutting men down and putting star players out of the game intentionally, he would soon be driven out of the League, probably on a stretcher.

When John Hummel of the Brooklyn club spiked Doyle in 1908, and greatly lessened the Giants' chances of winning the pennant, which the club ultimately lost, he came around to our clubhouse after the game and inquired for Larry. When he found how badly Doyle was cut, he was as broken up as any member of our team.

John Hummel, Brooklyn Superbas

"If I'd known I was goin' to cut you, Larry, I wouldn't have slid," he said.

"That's all right," answered Doyle. "I guess I was blockin' you."

Ballplayers don't say much in a situation of that kind. But each one who witnessed the incident knew that when Doyle doubled down, spiked, most of our chances of the pennant went down with him, for it broke up the infield of the team at a most important moment. It takes some time for a new part to work into a clock so that it keeps perfect time again, no matter how delicate is the workmanship of the new part. So the best infielder takes time to fit into the infield of a Big-League club and have it hit on all four cylinders again.

Fred Merkle is one of the few ballplayers who still prefers the head-first slide, and he sticks to it only on certain occasions. He is the best man to steal third base playing ball to-day. He declares that, when he is going into the bag, he can see better by shooting his headfirst and that he can swing his body away from the base and just hook it with one fingernail, leaving just that to touch. And he keeps his nails clipped short in the season, so that there is very little exposed to which the ball can be applied. If he sees that the third baseman is playing inside the bag, he goes behind it and hooks it with his finger, and if the man is playing back, he cuts through in front, pulling his body away from the play. But the common or garden variety of player will take the hook slide, feet first, because he can catch the bag with one leg, and the feet aren't as tender a portion of the anatomy to be roughly touched as the head and shoulders.

A club of base runners will do more to help a pitcher win than a batting order of hard hitters, I believe. Speed is the great thing in the baseball of to-day. By speed I do not mean that good men must be sprinters alone. They must be fast starters, fast runners, and fast thinkers. Remember that last one—fast thinkers.

Harry McCormick, formerly the leftfielder on the Giants, when he joined the club before his legs began to go bad, was a sprinter, one of the fastest men who ever broke into the League. Before he took up baseball as a profession, he had been a runner in college. But McCormick was never a brilliant base stealer because he could not get the start.

When a man is pitching for a club of base runners he knows that every time a player with a stealing reputation gets on and there is an outside chance of his scoring, the run is going to be hung up. The tallies give a pitcher confidence to proceed. Then, when the club has the reputation of possessing a great bunch of base runners, the other pitcher is worried all the time and has to devote about half his energies to watching the bases. This makes him easier to hit.

But put a hard hitter who is a slow base runner on the club, and he does little good. There used to be a man on the Giants, named "Charley" Hickman, who played third base and then the outfield. He was one of the best natural hitters who ever wormed his way into baseball, but when he got on, the bases were blocked. He could not run, and it took a hit to advance him a base. Get a fast man on behind him and, because the rules of the game do not permit one runner to pass another, it was like having a freight train preceding the Twentieth Century Limited on a single-track road. Hickman was not so slow when he first started, but after a while his legs went bad and his weight increased, so that he was built like a box car, to carry out the railroad figure.

Hickman finally dropped back into the minor leagues and continued to bat three hundred, but he had to lose the ball to make the journey clear around the bases on one wallop. Once he hit the old flagpole in center field at the Polo Grounds on the fly, and just did nose the ball out at the plate. It was a record hit for distance. At last, while still maintaining the three-hundred pace, Hickman was dropped by the Toledo club of the American Association.

"Charley" Hickman, New York Giants

"Why did you let Charley Hickman go?" I asked the manager one day.

"Because he was tyin' up traffic on the bases," he replied.

Merkle is not a particularly fast runner, but he is a great base stealer because he has acquired the knack of "getting away." He never tries to steal until he has his start. He is also a good arriver, as I have pointed out. It was like getting a steamroller in motion to start Hickman.

Clever ballplayers and managers are always trying to evolve new base-running tactics that will puzzle the other team, but "there ain't no new stuff."

It is a case of digging up the old ones. Pitchers are also earnest in their endeavors to discover improved ways to stop base running. Merkle and I worked out a play during the spring training season in 1911 which caught perhaps a dozen men off first base before the other teams began to watch for the trick. And it was not original with me. I got the idea from "Patsy" Flaherty, a Boston pitcher who has his salary wing fastened to his left side.

Flaherty would pitch over to first base quickly, and the fielder would shoot the ball back. Then Flaherty would pop one through to the batter, often catching him off his guard, and sneaking a strike over besides leaving the runner flat on the ground in the position

"Patsy" Flaherty, Boston Doves

in which he had been when he slid back to the bag. If the batter hit the ball, the runner was in no attitude to get a start, and, on an infield tap, it was easy to make a double play.

The next time that the man got on base, Flaherty would shoot the ball over to first as before, and the runner would be up on his feet and away from the bag, expecting him to throw it to the plate. But as the first baseman whipped it back quickly Flaherty returned the ball and the runner was caught flat footed and made to look foolish. Ballplayers do certainly hate to appear ridiculous, and the laugh from the crowd upsets a Big-Leaguer more than anything else, even a call from McGraw, because the crowd cannot hear that and does not know the man is looking foolish.

It was almost impossible to steal bases on "Patsy" Flaherty because he had the men hugging the bag all the time, and if he had had other essentials of a pitcher, he would have been a great one. He even lived in the Big-League for some time with this quick throw as his only asset.

I adopted the Flaherty movement, but it is harder for a right-hander to use, as he is not in such a good position to whip the ball to the bag. Merkle and I rehearsed it in spring practice. As soon as a man got on first base, I popped the ball over to Merkle, and without even making a stab at the runner, he shot it to me. Then back again, just as the runner had let go of the bag and was getting up. The theoretical result: He was caught flat-footed. Sometimes it worked. Then they began to play for me.

Another play on which the changes have often been rung is the double steal with men on first and third bases. That is McGraw's favorite situation in a crisis.

"Somebody's got to look foolish on the play," says "Mac," "and I don't want to furnish any laughs."

The old way to work it was to have the man on first start for second, as if he were going to make a straight steal. Then as soon as the catcher drew his arm back to throw, the runner on third started home. No Big-League club can have a look into the pennant set without trying to interrupt the journey of that man going to second in a tight place, because if no play is made for him and a hit follows, it nets the club two runs instead of one.

Most teams try to stop this play by having the shortstop or second baseman come in and take a short throw, and if the man on third breaks for home, the receiver of the ball whips it back. If both throws are perfect, the runner is caught at the plate.

But the catchers found that certain clubs were making this play in routine fashion, the runner on first starting with the pitch, and the one on third making his break just as soon as the catcher drew back his arm. Then the backstops began making a bluff throw to second and whipping the ball to third, often getting the runner by several feet, as he had already definitely started for the plate.

"Tommy" Leach, Pittsburgh Pirates

"Tommy" Leach of the Pittsburg club was probably caught oftener on this bluff throw than any other man in baseball. For some time, he had been making the play against clubs which used the short throw, and starting as the catcher drew back his arm, as that was the only chance he had to score. One day in the season of 1908, when the Pirates were playing against the Giants, Clarke was on first and Leach on third, with one run required to balance the game. McGraw knew the double steal was to be expected, as two were out. Bresnahan was aware of this, too.

McGinnity was pitching, and with his motion, Clarke got his start. Bresnahan drew back his arm as if to throw to second, and true to form, Leach was on his way to the plate. But Bresnahan had not let go of the ball, and he shot it to Devlin, Leach being run down in the base line and the Pittsburg club eventually losing the game.

Again, and again Leach fell for this bluff throw, until the news spread around the circuit that once a catcher drew back his arm with a man on first base and "Tommy" Leach on third, there would be no holding him on the bag. He was caught time and again—indeed as frequently as the play came up. It was his "groove." He could not be stopped from making his break. At last Clarke had to order him to abandon the play until he could cure himself of this self-starting habit.

"What you want to do on that play is cross 'em," is McGraw's theory, and he proceeded to develop the delayed steal with this intent.

Put the men back on first and third bases. Thank you. The pitcher has the ball. The runner on first intentionally takes too large a lead. The pitcher throws over, and he moves a few steps toward second. Then a few more. All that time the man on third is edging off an inch, two inches, a foot. The first baseman turns to throw to second to stop that man. The runner on third plunges for the plate, and usually gets there. It's a hard one to stop, but that's its purpose.

Then, again, it can be worked after the catcher gets the ball. The runner starts from first slowly and the catcher hesitates, not knowing whether to throw to first or second. Since the runner did not start with the pitch, theoretically no one has come in to take a short throw, and the play cannot be made back to the plate if the ball is thrown to second. This form of the play is usually successful.

Miller Huggins is one of the hardest second basemen in the League to work it against successfully. With men on first and third, he always comes in for the short throw on the chance and covers himself up.

After we had stolen our way to a pennant in the National League in the season of 1911, and after our five leading base runners had been "mugged" by the police in St. Louis so that the catchers would know them, many fans expected to see us steal a world's championship, and we half expected it ourselves.

But so did "Connie" Mack, and there lies the answer. He knew our strong point, and his players had discussed and rehearsed ways and means to break up our game. Mack had been watching the Giants for weeks previous to the series and had had his spies taking notes.

"We've got to stop them running bases," he told his men before the first game, I have learned since.

And they did. Guess the St. Louis police must have sent Thomas and Lapp copies of those pictures.

Mack's pitchers cut their motions down to nothing with men on the bases, microscopic motions, and they watched the runners like hawks. Thomas had been practicing to get the men. The first time that Devore made a break to steal, he was caught several feet from the bag.

"And you call yourself fast!" commented Collins as he threw the ball back to the pitcher and jogged to his job. "You remind me of a cop on a fixed post," he flung over his shoulder.

Pitchers have a great deal to do with the defensive efficiency of the club. If they do not hold the runners up, the best catcher in the world cannot stop them at their destination. That is the reason why so many high-class catchers have been developed by the Chicago Cubs. The team has always had a good pitching staff, and men like Overall, Brown and Reulbach force the runners to stick to the oases of safety.

Ed Reulbach, Chicago Cubs

The Giants stole their way to a pennant in 1911, and it wasn't on account of the speedy material, but because McGraw had spent days teaching his men to slide and emphasizing the necessity of getting the jump. Then he picked the stages of the game when the attempts to steal were to be made. But McGraw, with his all-star cast of thieves, was stopped in the world's series by one Cornelius McGillicuddy.

# Notable Instances Where the "Inside" Game Has Failed

*The "Inside" Game is of Little Avail when a Batter Knocks a Home Run with the Bases Full—Many Times the Strategies of Managers have Failed because Opposing Clubs "Doctored" their Grounds—"Rube" Waddell Once Cost the Athletics a Game by Failing to Show up after the Pitcher's Box had been Fixed for Him—But, although the "Inside" Game Sometimes Fails, no Manager Wants a Player who will Steal Second with the Bases Full.*

**THERE IS** an old story about an altercation which took place during a wedding ceremony in the backwoods of the Virginia mountains. The discussion started over the propriety of the best man holding the ring, and by the time that it had been finally settled the bride gazed around on a dead bridegroom, a dead father, and a dead best man, not to mention three or four very dead ushers and a clergyman.

"Them new-fangled self-cockin' automatic guns has sure raised hell with my prospects," she sighed.

That's the way I felt when John Franklin Baker popped that home run into the right-field stand in the ninth inning of the third game of the 1911 world's series with one man already out. For eight and one-third innings the Giants had played "inside" ball, and I had carefully nursed along every batter who came to the plate, studying his weakness and pitching at it. It looked as if we were going to win the game, and then zing! And also, zowie! The ball went into the stand on a line and I looked around at my fielders who had had the game almost within their grasp a minute before. Instantly, I realized that I had been pitching myself out, expecting the end to come in nine innings. My arm felt like so much lead hanging to my side after that hit. I wanted to go and get some crape and hang it on my salary whip.

Then that old story about the wedding popped into my head, and I said to myself: "He has sure raised hell with your prospects."

"Sam" Strang, the official pinch hitter of the Giants a few seasons ago, was one of the best in the business. McGraw sent him to the bat in the ninth inning of a game the Giants were playing in Brooklyn. We were two runs behind and two were already out, with one runner on the bases, and he was only as far as second. "Doc" Scanlan was pitching for Brooklyn, and, evidently intimidated by Sam's pinch-hitting reputation or something, suddenly became wild and gave the Giant batter three balls.

"Sam" Stang, New York Giants

With the count three and nothing, McGraw shouted from the bench: "Wait it out, Sam!"

But Sam did not hear him, and he took a nice masculine, virile, full-armed swing at the ball and fouled it out of the reach of all the local guardians of the soil.

"Are you deaf?" barked McGraw. "Wait it out, I tell you." As a matter of fact, Strang was a little deaf and did not hear the shouted instructions the second time. But "Doc" Scanlan was sensitive as to hearing and, feeling sure Strang would obey the orders of McGraw, thought he would be taking no chances in putting the next ball over the center of the plate. It came up the "groove," and Strang admired it as it approached. Then he took his swing, and the next place the ball touched was in the Italian district just over the right field fence. The hit tied the score.

"Doc" Scanlan, Brooklyn Superbas

McGraw met Strang at the plate, and instead of greeting him with shouts of approbation, exclaimed: "I ought to fine you $25, and would, except for those two runs and the few points' difference the game will make in the percentage. Come on now, boys. Let's win this one."

And we did in the eleventh inning.

That was a case of the "inside" game failing. Any Big-League pitcher with brains would have laid the ball over after hearing McGraw shout earnest and direct orders at the batter to "wait it out." Scanlan was playing the game and Strang was not, but it broke for Sam. It was the first time in his life that he ever hit the ball over the right field fence in Brooklyn, and he has never done it since. If he had not been lucky in connecting with that ball and lifting it where it did the most good, his pay envelope would have been lighter by $25 at the end of the month, and he would have obtained an accurate idea of McGraw's opinion of his intellectuality.

In the clubhouse after the victory, McGraw said: "Honest, Sam, why did you swing at that ball after I had told you not to?"

"I didn't hear you," replied Strang.

"Well, it's lucky you hit it where they weren't," answered McGraw, "because if any fielder had connected with the ball, there would have been a rough greeting waiting for you on the bench. And as a tip, Sam, direct from me: You got away with it once, but don't try it again. It was bad baseball."

"But that straight one looked awful good to me coming up the 'groove,'" argued Sam.

"Don't fall for all the good lookers, Sam," suggested McGraw, the philosopher.

Strang is now abroad having his voice cultivated and he intends to enter the grand-opera field as soon as he can finish the spring training in Paris and get his throat into shape for the Big-League music circuit. But I will give any orchestra leader who faces Sam a tip. If he doesn't want him to come in strong where the music is marked "rest," don't put one in the "groove," because Strang just naturally can't help swinging at it. He is a poor waiter.

The Boston club lost eighteen straight games in the season of 1910, and as the team was leaving the Polo Grounds after having dropped four in a row, making the eighteen, I said to Tenney: "How does it seem, Fred, to be on a club that has lost eighteen straight?"

"It's what General Sherman said war is," replied Tenney, who seldom swears. "But for all-around entertainment I would like to see John McGraw on a team which had dropped fifteen or sixteen in a row."

As if Tenney had put the curse on us, the Giants hit a losing streak the next day that totaled six games straight. Everything that we tried broke against us. McGraw would attempt the double steal, and both throws would be accurate, and the runner caught at the plate. A hit and a run sign would be given, and the batter would run up against a pitch-out.

McGraw was slowly going crazy. All his pet "inside" tricks were worthless. He, the king of baseball clairvoyants, could not guess right. It began to look to me as if Tenney would get his entertainment.

After the sixth one had gone against us and McGraw had not spoken a friendly word to any one for a week, he called the players around him in the clubhouse.

"I ought to let you all out and get a gang of high-school boys in here to defend the civic honor of this great and growing city whose municipal pride rests on your shoulders," he said. "But I'm not going to do it. Hereafter we will cut out all 'inside' stuff and play straight baseball. Every man will go up there and hit the ball just as you see it done on the lots."

Into this oration was mixed a judicious amount of sulphur. The Cubs had just taken the first three of a four-game series from us without any trouble at all. The next day we went out and resorted to the wallop, plain, untrimmed slugging tactics, and beat Chicago 17 to 1. Later we returned to the hand-raised, cultivated hot-house form of baseball, but for a week we played the old-fashioned game with a great deal of success. It changed our luck.

Another method which has upset the "inside" game of many visiting teams is "doping" the grounds.

The first time in my baseball career that I ever encountered this was in Brooklyn when Hanlon was the manager. Every time he thought I was going to pitch there; he would have the diamond doctored for me in the morning. The ground-keeper sank the pitcher's box down so that it was below the level of all the bases instead of slightly elevated as it should be.

Hanlon knew that I used a lot of speed when I first broke into the League, getting some of it from my elevation on the diamond. He had a team of fast men who depended largely on a bunting game and their speed in getting to first base to win. With me fielding bunts out of the hollow, they had a better chance of making their goal.

Then pitching from the lower level would naturally result in the batters getting low balls, because I would be more apt to misjudge the elevation of the plate. Low ones were made to bunt. Finally, Hanlon always put into the box to work against me a little pitcher who was not affected as much as I by the topographical changes.

George Davis, New York Giants

"Why," I said to George Davis, the Giants' manager, the first time I pitched out of the cellar which in Brooklyn was regarded as the pitcher's box, "I'm throwing from a hollow instead of off a mound."

"Sure," replied Davis. "They 'doped' the grounds for you. But never mind. When we are entertaining, the box at the Polo Grounds will be built up the days you are going to pitch against Brooklyn, and you can burn them over and at their heads if you like."

The thing that worried the Athletics most before the last world's series was the reputation of the Giants as base stealers. When we went to Philadelphia for the first game, I was surprised at the heavy condition of the base lines.

"Did it rain here last night?" I inquired from a native.

"No," he answered.

Then I knew that the lines had been wet down to slow up our fast runners and make it harder for them to steal. As things developed, this precaution was unnecessary, but it was an effort to break up what was known to be our strongest "inside" play.

Baseball men maintain that the acme of doctoring grounds was the work of the old Baltimore Orioles. The team was composed of fast men who were brilliant bunters and hard base runners. The soil of the infield was mixed with a form of clay which, when wet and then rolled, was almost as hard as concrete. The ground outside the first and third base lines was built up slightly to keep well placed bunts from rolling foul, while toward first base there was a distinct down grade to aid the runner in reaching that station with all possible expedition. Toward second there was a gentle slope, and it was downhill to third. But coming home from third was up-hill work. A player had to be a mountain climber to make it. This all benefited fast men like Keeler, McGraw,

Kelley and Jennings whose most dangerous form of attack was the bunt.

The Orioles did not stop at doctoring the infield. The grass in the outfield was permitted to grow long and was unkempt. Centre and left fields were kept level, but in right field there was a sharp down grade to aid the fast Keeler. He had made an exhaustive study of all the possible angles at which the ball might bound and had certain paths that he followed, but which were not marked out by signposts for visiting right-fielders. He was sure death on hits to his territory, while usually wallops got past visiting right-fielders. And so great was the grade that "Wee Willie" was barely visible from the batter's box. A hitting team coming to Baltimore would be forced to fall into the bunting game or be entirely outclassed. And the Orioles did not furnish their guests with topographical maps of the grounds either.

"Wee Willie" Keeler, New York Giants

The habit of doctoring grounds is not so much in vogue now as it once was. For a long time, it was considered fair to arrange the home field to the best advantage of the team which owned it, for otherwise what was the use in being home? It was on the same principle that a general builds his breastworks to best suit the fighting style of his army, for they are his breastworks.

But lately among the profession, sentiment and baseball legislation have prevailed against the doctoring of grounds, and it is done very little. Occasionally a pitching box is raised or lowered to meet the requirements of a certain man, but they are not altered every day to fit the pitcher, as they once were. Such tactics often hopelessly upset the plan of battle of the visiting club unless this exactly coincided with the habits of the home team. Many strategic plans have been wasted on carefully arranged grounds, and many "inside" plays have gone by the boards when the field was fixed so that a bunt was bound to roll foul if the ball followed the laws of gravitation, as it usually does, because the visiting team was known to have the bunting habit.

A good story of doctored grounds gone wrong is told of the Philadelphia Athletics. The eccentric "Rube" Waddell had bundles of speed in his early days, and from a slightly elevated pitcher's box the batter could scarcely identify "Rube's" delivery from that of a cannon. He was scheduled to pitch one day and showed around at morning practice looking unusually fit for George.

"How are you feeling to-day, George?" asked "Connie" Mack, his boss.

"Never better," replied the light-hearted "Rube."

"Well, you work this afternoon."

"All right," answered Waddell.

Then the ground-keeper got busy and built the pitcher's box up about two feet, so that Waddell would have a splendid opportunity to cut loose all his speed. At that time, he happened to be the only tall man on the pitching staff of the Philadelphia club, and, as a rule, the box was kept very low. The scheme would probably have worked out as planned, if it had not been that Waddell, in the course of his noon-day wanderings, met several friends in whose society he became so deeply absorbed that he neglected to report at the ballpark at all. He also forgot to send word, and here was the pitcher's box standing up out of the infield like one of the peaks of the Alps.

As the players gathered, and Waddell failed to show up, the manager nervously looked at his watch. At last, he sent out scouts to the "Rube's" known haunts, but no trace of the temperamental artist could be found. The visitors were already on the field, and it was too late to lower the box. A short pitcher had to work in the game from this peak of progress, while the opposing team installed a skyscraper on the mound. The Philadelphia club was badly beaten and Waddell heavily fined for his carelessness in disrupting the "inside" play of his team. An old and favorite trick used to be to soap the soil around the pitcher's box, so that when a man was searching for some place to dry his perspiring hands and grabbed up this soaped earth, it made his palm slippery and he was unable to control the ball.

Of course, the home talent knew where the good ground lay and used it or else carried some unadulterated earth in their trousers' pockets, as a sort of private stock. But our old friend "Bugs" Raymond hit on a scheme to spoil this idea and make the trick useless. Arthur always perspired profusely when he pitched, and several managers, perceiving this, had made it a habit to soap the dirt liberally whenever it was his turn to work. While he was pitching for St. Louis, he went into the box against the Pirates one day in Pittsburg. His hands were naturally slippery, and several times he had complained that he could not dry them in the dirt, especially in Pittsburg soil.

As Raymond worked in the game in question, he was noticed, particularly by the Pittsburg batters and spectators, to get better as he went along. Frequently, his hand slipped into his back pocket, and then his control was wonderful. Sometimes, he would reach down and apparently pick up a handful of earth, but it did no damage. After the game, he walked over to Fred Clarke, and reached into his back pocket. His face broke into a grin.

"Ever see any of that stuff, Fred?" he asked innocently, showing the Pittsburg manager a handful of a dark brown substance. "That's rosin. It's great—lots better than soaped ground. Wish you'd keep a supply out there in the box for me when I'm going to work instead of that slippery stuff you've got out there now. Will you, as a favor to me?"

Thereafter, all the pitchers got to carrying rosin or pumice stone in their pockets, for the story quickly went round the circuit, and it is useless to soap the soil in the box anymore. There are many tricks by which the grounds or ball are "fixed," but for nearly all an antidote has been discovered, and these questionable forms of the "inside" game have failed so often that they have largely been abandoned.

One Big-League manager used always to give his men licorice or some other dark and adhesive and juicy substance to chew on a dingy day. The purpose was to dirty the ball so that it was harder for the batters to see when the pitcher used his fast one. As soon as a new ball was thrown into the game, it was quickly passed around among the fielders, and instead of being the lily-white thing that left the umpire's hands, when it finally got to the pitcher's box it was a very pronounced brunette. But some eagle-eyed arbiter detected this and kept pouring new balls into the game when the non-licorice chewers were at the bat, while he saved the discolored ones for the consumption of the masticators. It was another trick that failed.

Frequently, backgrounds are tampered with if the home club is notably weak at the bat. The best background for a batter is a dull, solid green. Many clubs have painted backgrounds in several contrasting, broken colors so that the sunlight, shining on them, blinds the batter. The Chicago White Sox are said to have done this, and for many years the figures showed that the batting of both the Chicago players and the visitors at their park was very light. The White Sox's hitting was weak anywhere, so that the poor background was an advantage to them. Injuries have often upset the "inside" play of a club.

Usually, a team's style revolves around one or two men, and the taking of them out of the game destroys the whole machine. The substitute does not think as quickly; neither does he see and grasp the opportunities as readily. This was true of the Cubs last season. Chance and Evers used to be the "inside" game of the team. Evers was out of the game most of the summer and Chance was struck in the head with a pitched ball and had to quit. The playing of the Chicago team fell down greatly as a result.

Chance is the sort of athlete who is likely to get injured. When he was a catcher, he was always banged up because he never got out of the way of anything. He is that kind of player. If he has to choose between accepting a pair of spikes in a vital part of his anatomy and getting a put-out, or dodging the spikes and losing the put-out, he always takes the put-out and usually the spikes. He never dodges away from a ball when at bat that may possibly break over the plate and cost him a strike. That is why he was hit in the head. He lingered too long to ascertain whether the ball was going to curve and found out that it was not, which put him out of the game, the Cubs practically out of the pennant race, and broke up their "inside" play.

Roger Bresnahan is the same kind of a man. He thinks quickly, and is a brilliant player, but he never dodges anything. He is often hurt as a result. Once, when he was with the Giants, he was hit in the face with a pitched ball, and McGraw worried while he was laid up, for fear that it would make him bat shy. After he came back, he was just as friendly with the plate as ever. The injury of men like Chance and Bresnahan, whose services are of such vital importance to the "inside" play of a team, destroys the effectiveness of the club.

Once, in 1908, when we were fighting the Cubs for the pennant at every step, McGraw planned a bunting game against Overall, who is big and not very fast in covering the little rollers. Bresnahan and O'Day had been having a serial argument through two games, and Roger, whose nerves were worn to a frazzle, like those of the rest of us at that time, thought "Hank" had been shading his judgment slightly toward the Cubs.

In another story I have pointed out that O'Day, the umpire, was stubborn and that nothing could be gained by continually picking on him.

When the batteries were announced for that game, McGraw said as the team went to the field: "We can beat this guy Overall by bunting."

Bresnahan went out to put on his chest protector and shin guards. O'Day happened to be adjusting his makeup near him.

Roger could not resist the temptation.

"Why don't you put on a Chicago uniform, 'Hank', instead of those duds?" he asked. "Is it true, if the Cubs win the pennant, they've promised to elect you alderman in Chicago?"

"Get out of the game and off the field," said O'Day.

Bresnahan had to obey the injunction and Needham, the only other available catcher, went behind the mat.

"Tom" Needham never beat out a bunt in his life, and he destroyed all McGraw's plans because, with him in the game instead of Bresnahan, the style had to be switched. We lost. Bresnahan, a fast man and a good bunter batted third and would have been valuable in the attack best adapted to beat Overall. But his sudden demise and the enforced substitution of the plodding Needham ruined the whole plan of campaign. Therefore, frequently umpires upset a team's "inside" game.

"Tom" Needham, Chicago Cubs

One of McGraw's schemes back-fired on him when Luderus, the hard-hitting Philadelphia first baseman, broke into the League. Someone had tipped "Mac" off, and tipped him wrong, that this youngster could be disconcerted in a pinch by the catcher discussing signs and what-not with him, thus distracting his attention.

"Chief," said McGraw before the game, "if this Luderus gets up in a tight place, slip him a little talk."

The situation came, and Meyers obeyed instructions. The game was in Philadelphia, and three men were on the bases with two out. Ames was pitching.

"What are you bringing the bat up with you for?" asked the "Chief" as Luderus arranged himself at the plate.

No answer.

Then Meyers gave Ames his sign. Next, he fixed his fingers in a fake signal and addressed the young batter.

Fred Luderus, Philadelphia Phillies

"The best hitters steal signs," said the "Chief." "Just look down in my glove and see the signals."

But Luderus was not caught and kept his eyes glued on Ames. He hit the next ball over the right field wall and won the game.

As he crossed the plate, he said to the "Chief": "It's too easy. I don't need your signs. They pulled that one on me in the bushes long ago."

"After this, when that fellow bats," said McGraw to Meyers later, "do as exact an imitation of the sphinx as you know how. The tip was no good."

The trick of talking to the hitter is an old one. The idea is for the catcher to give a wrong sign, for his benefit, after having flashed the right one, induce the batter, usually a youngster, to look down at it, and then have the pitcher shoot one over the plate while he is staring in the glove. "Steve" Evans, the St. Louis right-fielder, tells a story of a fan who sat in the same box at the Cardinals' park every day and devoted most of his time to roasting him (S. Evans). His favorite expressions in connection with Evans were "bone dead," "wooden head," and so on. He loudly claimed that "Steve" had no knowledge of the game and spoiled every play that Bresnahan tried to put through.

One day, when the Giants were playing in St. Louis, someone knocked up a high foul which landed in this orator's box. He saw it coming, tried to dodge, used poor judgment, and, realizing that the ball was going to strike him, snatched his hat off, and took it full on an immodestly bald head.

"Steve" Evans was waiting to go to the bat. He shifted his chew to his other cheek and exclaimed in a voice that could not have been heard more than two miles away: "That's the 'gink' who has been calling me a 'bone head.'"

"Steve" got a great laugh from the crowd, but right there the St. Louis club lost a patron, for the bald-headed one has never been seen at the grounds since, according to Evans, and his obituary has not been printed yet, either.

"Al" Bridwell, formerly the Giants' shortstop, was one of the cleverest men at the "inside" game that ever broke into the Big-Leagues, and it was this that made him valuable. Then suddenly his legs went bad, and he slowed up. It was his speed and his ability to bunt and his tireless waiting at the plate to make all toilers in the box pitch that had made him a great player. He seldom swung at a bad ball. As soon as he slowed up, McGraw knew he would have to go if the Giants were to win the pennant. He deeply regretted letting the gritty, little shortstop, whose legs had grown stiff in his service, leave the club, but sentiment never won any pennants.

"Al," he said to Bridwell, "I'm going to let you go to Boston. Your legs will be all right eventually, but I've got to have a fast man now while you are getting back your old speed."

"That's all right, 'Mac,'" replied Bridwell. "It's all part of the game."

He did not rave and swear that he had been double-crossed, as many players do under the same circumstances. I never heard Bridwell swear, and I never found anyone else who did. He had been playing for weeks, when every time he moved it pained him, because he thought he might have a share of the money that winning a pennant would mean. It was a staggering blow to him, this sending him from a pennant possibility to a hopeless tail-ender, but he took it gamely.

"I guess I was 'gumming' the inside stuff," he said.

And he did get some of the prize money. The boys voted him a share.

It will be seen that the "inside" game sometimes fails. Many a time I have passed a catcher or good batter to take a chance on a pitcher, and then have had him make a hit just when hits were not at all welcome. I walked a catcher once and had the pitcher shove the ball over first base for a single, when he closed his eyes and dodged back in an effort to get his head out of the line, he thought it was pursuing before it curved. In ducking, he got his bat in front of the ball, a result he had never obtained with his eyes open.

Once I started to pass "Hans" Wagner in a pinch to take a chance on the next batter and was a little careless in throwing the ball too close to the plate. He reached out and slapped it for a single. Again the "inside" game had failed.

Speaking pretty generally, most managers prefer to use this "inside" game, though, and there are few vacancies in the Big-Leagues right now for the man who is liable to steal second with the bases full.

# Pitching In A Pinch

*By Hall of Fame Pitcher, Christy Mathewson*

As told first-hand dating back to Major League Baseball in the early 1900's with fascinating stories, insights, and quotes from his playing days including iconic stars Honus Wagner, Ty Cobb, Fred Clarke, Joe Tinker, "Johnny" Evers, "Chief" Meyers, "Rube" Marquard, Mordecai "Three Finger" Brown, Grover Cleveland Alexander, Orvie Overall, Ed Delahanty, "Rube" Waddell, "Slim" Sallee, "Home Run" Baker, and many other players, plus legendary Managers John McGraw and Connie Mack.

**With 100 Ballplayer Photos Added!**

1912 Revised Edition

Published by Baseball Classics™

Foreword by Baseball Classics Founder
# DEAN PATINO

Made in the USA
Columbia, SC
27 June 2024

e534434f-367f-4e65-925e-d88d01bc45faR01